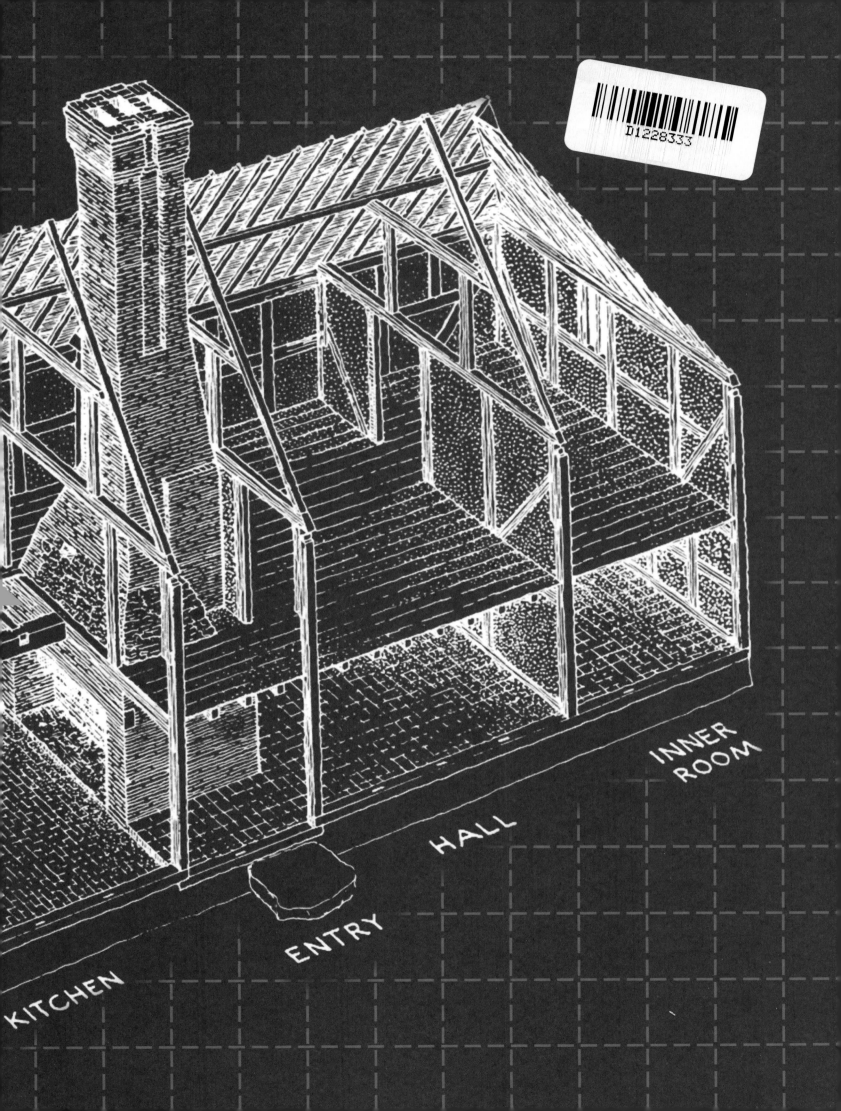

KITCHEN

ENTRY

HALL

INNER
ROOM

The Evolution of the Cape Cod House:
AN ARCHITECTURAL HISTORY

FRONT DOOR ELEVATION

Arthur P. Richmond

4880 Lower Valley Road Atglen, Pennsylvania 19310

Other Schiffer Books By The Author:

Cape Cod Lighthouses and Lightships,
    978-0-7643-3545-7, $45.00

Gingerbread Gems: Victorian Architecture of Oak Bluffs,
    978-0-7643-2682-0, $29.95

Other Schiffer Books on Related Subjects:

New England's Architecture by Wallace Nutting,
    978-0-7643-2654-7, $29.95

Saltbox and Cape Cod Houses. Stanley Schuler,
    978-0-7643-0998-6, $29.95

Library of Congress Control Number: 2011931541

Designed by Stephanie Daugherty
Type set inHehenHebTBol/Minion Pro/Gill Sans Std
ISBN: 978-0-7643-3848-9
Printed in China

Schiffer Books are available at special discounts for bulk purchases for sales promotions or premiums. Special editions, including personalized covers, corporate imprints, and excerpts can be created in large quantities for special needs. For more information contact the publisher:

Schiffer Publishing Ltd.
4880 Lower Valley Road
Atglen, PA 19310
Phone: (610) 593-1777
Fax: (610) 593-2002
E-mail: Info@schifferbooks.com

For the largest selection of fine reference books on this and related subjects, please visit our website at

www.schifferbooks.com

We are always looking for people to write books on new and related subjects. If you have an idea for a book, please contact us at proposals@schifferbooks.com

This book may be purchased from the publisher. Include $5.00 for shipping. Please visit your bookstore first. You may write for a free catalog.

In Europe, Schiffer books are distributed by
Bushwood Books
6 Marksbury Ave.
Kew Gardens
Surrey TW9 4JF England
Phone: 44 (0) 20 8392 8585
Fax: 44 (0) 20 8392 9876
E-mail: info@bushwoodbooks.co.uk
Website: www.bushwoodbooks.co.uk

This book is dedicated to family. Not only mine, but to all individuals past and present who have lived in the houses illustrated in this book. The house in the adjacent image is where my 12th great-grandfather was born in 1594 in Ashton-Keynes, England.

Contents

Preface

This book has been both a new and exciting learning experience for me. My previous books, in particular the highly popular WIDE series, have concentrated on photographing popular picturesque vistas without a serious discussion or description of a specific topic.

My book *Harbors of Cape Cod and the Islands,* which included text of a historical nature, was extensive and comprehensive, although relatively easy to put together. Subsequently, *Lighthouses and Lightships of Cape Cod* required extensive research, including trips to the Washington, D.C., area to visit the National Archives and the United States Coast Guard's Historian's Office; but there are only a discrete number of lights (just five on the Vineyard). The parameters of that project were defined and relatively easy to organize.

On the other hand, this book was fraught with numerous organizational decisions. Considering that in the mid-1800s there were more than two thousand houses built and standing in this architectural style, how do you then go about selecting which ones to study and photograph? Two basic approaches that could have been taken would be to select houses by towns, such as Eastham, Wellfleet, and Truro, or to arrange the houses by their style as half Cape, three-quarter Cape, or full Cape. I could have also approached the topic by arranging the homes in terms of their age, starting with the oldest first. There are problems with that method because the dating of a specific property in many cases is highly speculative.

So, what did I do? With no formal training in architecture, I first looked for sources of information regarding old Cape Cod homes in this architectural style. There are three major and significant resources available to the researcher. The first is the Library of Congress and within it the Historic American Building Survey (HABS), which in the 1930s catalogued, collected data, drew plans, and photographed thousands (almost 40,000 to date) of properties across the country. Not applicable to this project, there is also the Historic American Engineering Record (HAER), which concentrated and completed the same information on industrial properties, and the Historic American Landscapes Survey (HALS). One simply has to go on-line and search the Library of Congress website for one's topic of interest. This was my first and major source of information. I could select homes that were studied in detail eighty years ago and I would have valuable information that could be used. Images and plans of the properties before renovation and modernization provide a comparison of the properties as they exist in the twenty-first century. Unfortunately, some of the houses are no longer standing.

Also, in conjunction with the National Park Service and specifically, the creation of the Cape Cod National Seashore, (CCNS) properties within the boundaries of the future park were investigated and copious details were collected about fifty years ago. Several of the houses detailed in this book were also studied at that time by qualified professionals, including historical architects.

My other source of information is data collected by representatives in each community who recorded information on Form B for the Massachusetts Historical Commission (MHC). These forms from the MHC can be found in each town,

usually available at the community library. Information from town records, as well as other sources, is listed on the Form B for the researcher.

My third source of information was from individuals, either as owners of specific properties that they were familiar with as a docent at a museum property. Several of the homes described in this book are museums and are open to the public during certain seasons.

This is a book about a specific architectural style—the one-and-a-half-story house with a steep gable roof that we call a Cape. Numerous Capes, found on the following pages, are photographed and described, some in detail. This book does not identify each house in relation to the evolution of different architectural styles through the centuries. A basic background of early house styles and their designation is as follows:

Early- to mid-colonial (1620-1700): From the first colonists, English (Cape Cod), Dutch, (New York), French, and Spanish houses were built based on tradition from the old country.

Late colonial (1700-1720): Modifications and adaptations to the earlier homes to improve lifestyle.

Georgian (1720-1780): Large houses or mansions built based on English architecture; patterns (house plans) and architects became common.

The following are often referred to as post-colonial:

Federal (1780-1820): Classical, lacking detail found in Georgian homes and avoiding English influence.

Greek revival (1820-1840): Based on Greek temples with the use of pillars and pilasters, more common in larger houses and buildings.

Victorian (1830-1900): Built with the aid of machines, ornate, pretentious, and large with high ceilings.

This is a very brief account of American architectural development; the years are only approximations, as there was a considerable overlap in styles. It should be noted that the Cape Cod house discussed in this book is a basic utilitarian structure, and its fabric changed little through the years. Builders and/or owners, particularly on Cape Cod, may have added fancy trim around the doors in the eighteenth century (Georgian), but for the most part this was a limited occurrence.

Completing this project has been both satisfying and frustrating. I hope the reader benefits from viewing all the homes that are within these pages. And, for all the properties that are illustrated here, there are many more that could have been considered and included. The reader should be left with the thought that this house style, which can be traced back centuries, is a significant stage in American architecture.

Acknowledgments

With each book that has come to fruition, it seems that I am indebted to more and more people for their assistance in helping me complete the project. When I first started photographing the individual homes for this book, I kept detailed records and would use those to acknowledge and graciously thank them for their assistance. What became obvious though was that because many of these homes hold significant historical importance, the owners requested anonymity; they didn't want the notoriety of being identified as having a special property. To all the owners of the houses I visited, a warm and heartfelt, thank you. Each house within the book is identified by the original owner (if it's known), year it was built, and the town where it is located. Many of the houses in the book are specifically identified as museums and are open to the public for a small donation.

Many people have been of assistance in helping me research these houses. To the librarians and staffs of the Orleans, Eastham, Wellfleet, Truro, and Provincetown Libraries, thank you for your valuable assistance and advice. To all the individuals at the Eastham and Wellfleet Historical Societies who have helped me examine the past, thank you. To, as always, my in-house editor, Tony Pane, who continues to help me to learn how to write well, a very large thank you. And last, but not least, Carol, who is constantly providing insight and direction.

While most of the information found within this book has been documented and located at reliable sources, any error of commission or omission is mine. Every attempt has been made to ensure that details about these houses are correct; if not, the fault is mine.

Introduction

The title of this book provides the reader with an incomplete anticipation of the subject material found in these pages. It is not only about a house style, but also about a home where people have lived, worked, played, and died. In addition to being about the architectural fashion of the earliest colonists in New England, and more particularly about Cape Cod, this book also explores the history of the Cape Cod house through the generations that began more than twelve centuries ago in Great Britain, Holland, and Germany. In America, for nearly four hundred years, this structural style has stood the test of time and is not only one of America's most easily recognized dwellings, but also one of its most popular and familiar designs. Early in the eighteenth century, before the advent of "patterns" (house plans) and before the use of architects, the Cape Cod house was simply built using basic dimensions outlined in a contract between the builder and the future homeowner. From the time the Pilgrims first landed in Provincetown, explored what is now the outer Cape, and then sailed across the bay to settle in Plymouth, housing was an important necessity for survival. Their first permanent structures may be very similar to what is now found in Plimoth Plantation, a restoration and re-creation of a mid-1620s English farming village that may have had as many as three dozen houses and more than one hundred and sixty colonists.

Our narrative commences on the continent in England, where we visit a variety of old cottages and museums in order to observe evidence, with numerous photographs, of the succession of the different structural and functional aspects involving the Cape Cod house design. We begin our investigation with how the timber-framed homes evolved, beginning in the eighth century with its pole-like crucks, to the development of the king post, and then eventually to the queen post gable design. From the restoration of houses constructed centuries ago, we can see how walls were filled with a variety of materials during the reconstruction process. Necessary for heating and cooking, we examine and briefly explore the locations within the house of fireplaces and the corresponding essential chimney. Openings in the house, doors and windows, are considered next. We conclude our discussion with a wide range of images showing present day dwellings which might offer insight into what may have been the homes familiar to the earliest colonists.

Our journey continues to the New World, where we visit Plimoth Plantation and examine a re-created village that according to research may be replicas of the dwellings that the Pilgrims inhabited in 1627. Less than a century later and with hundreds of homes constructed across southeastern Massachusetts and Cape Cod, we identify the characteristics of a traditional Cape Cod house. The differences among a half house, three-quarter house, and a full house are described, and archetypal classic floor plans are presented and discussed. We then visit a selection of houses that have been maintained as museums where we are able to observe not only the exterior features but the interior furnishings that in several cases have been restored to a specific historical period. We finish by examining numerous cottages, primarily but not exclusively on Cape Cod, that have been restored, repaired, remodeled, and lovingly maintained by their owners. Enjoy.

This view is at the Weald and Downland Open Air Museum (WDOAM) with its centuries old buildings and homes in the distance. Located near Chichester, England, the museum features more than forty buildings that have been saved from destruction and faithfully restored. Some of the buildings were originally built more than five centuries ago (*used with permission of WDOAM*).

This image, more than a century old, illustrates a pair of Cape Cod houses on the rolling hills of the Outer Cape in Wellfleet, Massachusetts. In the distance are the nearby kettle ponds that were formed by the retreating glaciers thousands of years ago (*courtesy of WHS*).

Sixteenth-Century England

We begin our journey on the evolution and origin of the Cape Cod style house in England. When I thought I would be able to find a typical house that the colonists had lived in prior to coming to the New World, a search through the countryside of East Anglia and southeast England was less than fruitful. I never expected to find a specific house, but I thought that I might be able to find a cottage that best represented the theme of this book. If this book were about castles or ecclesiastical buildings, there would have been little or no difficulty. Much has been written and there are numerous books available to those interested about those specific subjects. Instead what has been described or identified by some authorities as "minor domestic architecture," cottages built by yeomen and tradesmen without any specifically designed plans, do not exist and are really not found in any location except in museums. For a variety of reasons, including their small size, the presence of more modern additions, their dismantling, or more drastic renovations that have occurred through the years, my search found that these cottages do not exist today. In fact it wasn't until the early 1900s that the architectural subject of these dwellings provoked enough interest that books would be written.

Our story begins about four hundred and fifty years ago after the end of the Tudor reign when England was changing from buildings with moats and fortifications to a more agrarian society where individuals and families could build cottages, providing they had four acres of land. Examine the accompanying images for examples of the following discussion. From 1550 to 1630, there was a building boom across the countryside, and many of these simple cottages were built. Since timber was abundant in the nearby forest, the house could be constructed using readily available materials. Dating from as early as the eighth century, the simplest type of framing involved two curved poles called crucks that would either be attached or held together by a ridge pole. The earliest of these primitive structures were circular and could have been more than twenty feet in diameter. There were no windows on these dwellings and the first door may have been a small opening, less than three feet high, covered by an animal pelt or a flat arrangement of wood that was simply pushed out. There was no chimney or an opening in the roof because any rain would enter and put out the fire. Smoke would eventually work its way out through the thatch. Eventually, the shape became rectangular with rounded ends. The length of the cottage would be determined by how many pairs of crucks were used. Through the years, tie-beams would be used to connect a cruck on one side to the cruck on the other side to provide additional support. For hundreds of years, until the eighteenth century in some rural areas of England, cruck construction would be used to build cottages and barns. Some still exist today and can be found throughout the United Kingdom as well as other countries on the continent.

Compare these two images of the Boarhunt Hall that was built originally in the fourteenth century. The black and white image shows the building before it was dismantled: the earliest hall is to the rear with a more recent addition to the front; at some point in time, chimneys had been added to the dwelling. The present-day image, restored on the grounds of the Weald and Downland Open Air Museum, shows how the hall may have looked when it was first built. Notice the curved supports on the sides of the end wall (*courtesy of WDOAM*).

Drive the back roads of England and you will find numerous old historic villages with timber frame houses, many of them two-story, but you will find very few that we think of as having a traditional Cape Cod style house design. This cottage, in the village of Thaxted, near Cambridge, is seen infrequently in the countryside villages. Located at the end of a city block and on the corner of a street, this dwelling reminds us of what a Cape Cod house might look like. Notice the large addition to the rear.

This thatched cottage restored on the grounds of the Weald and Downland Open Air Museum was probably built in the thirteenth century. It was later abandoned between 1348 and 1350, when the Black Death contributed to a decline in the town's population. What you see here in the reconstruction is only conjecture, as some of the houses in the town were timber framed and had roofs made of slate or tile instead of the thatch (*courtesy of WDOAM*).

The building of timber-framed cottages, referred to by architects as post and truss construction, reached its zenith in the sixteenth century, when the supply of wood was more than adequate. There is no intention in this book to discuss specific framing details as they evolved through the years; but it can be surmised that the earliest colonists to the New World were familiar with this form of cottage construction. Door and window openings evolved through the years. Windows were originally small openings with a shutter-like board held up by a short bar that could be dropped down, but that cut off the supply of light. Vertical bars of wood were then used, but it was found that diamond-shaped bars were better at preventing rain from entering the cottage. Inside, sliding shutters were also developed that would allow the window to open only partially. Glass would not be commonly available until the 1700s. The most primitive door, called a batten, was made of several vertical boards that were pegged to several horizontal boards. The finest and oldest examples of these doors in England were found in the most important building in the town—the church. These types of primitive doors can be seen in the New World as relatively common restorations on Capes. Throughout England, although there may be regional variations in the construction techniques and design, there are still a number of these buildings still standing. When Myles Standish and the *Mayflower* with her passengers sailed to the New World, some of the individuals aboard were familiar with building these cottages. When they landed in Plimouth Bay, the colonists were aware that they needed to eventually build shelters, and these were based on what had been built in their home country.

Found in a village just south of Sudbury, England, is this present day thatch cottage. It is possible to see the curve to the roof, which is also found on houses in the New World.

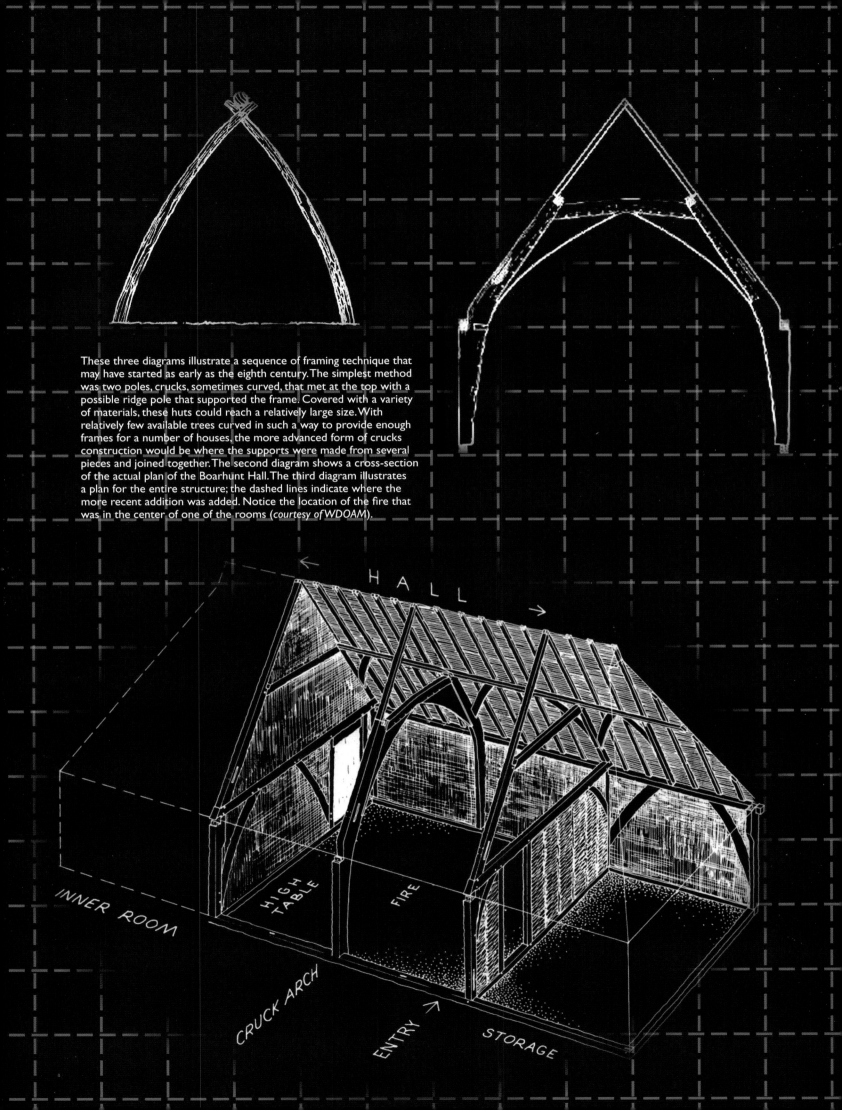

These three diagrams illustrate a sequence of framing technique that may have started as early as the eighth century. The simplest method was two poles, crucks, sometimes curved, that met at the top with a possible ridge pole that supported the frame. Covered with a variety of materials, these huts could reach a relatively large size. With relatively few available trees curved in such a way to provide enough frames for a number of houses, the more advanced form of crucks construction would be where the supports were made from several pieces and joined together. The second diagram shows a cross-section of the actual plan of the Boarhunt Hall. The third diagram illustrates a plan for the entire structure; the dashed lines indicate where the more recent addition was added. Notice the location of the fire that was in the center of one of the rooms (*courtesy of WDOAM*).

HALL

INNER ROOM

HIGH TABLE

FIRE

CRUCK ARCH

ENTRY

STORAGE

A present day interior view of the hall with the distinctive supporting cruck to the right (*permission of WDOAM*).

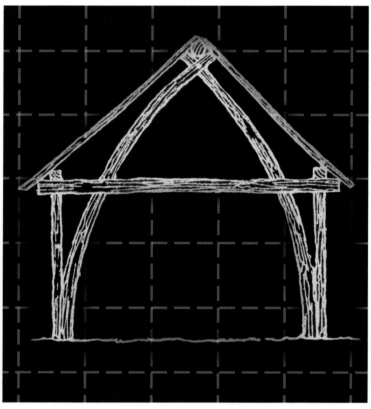

Compare this diagram and a brightly colored house in rural England. An intermediary step in the framing process not only involved the crucks but a set of posts that supported a cross beam and the rafters. Eventually the crucks would be eliminated.

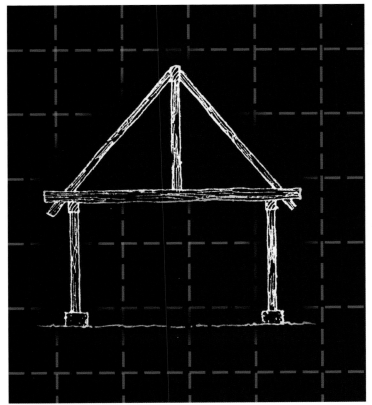

It was necessary to support the roof, and the next step in the construction method was the development of the king post, a central vertical beam that stood on a cross beam and extended to the top of the roofline. Found not only on the gable ends of the house, these sometimes ornate posts were located along the length of the house or barn as required. The present day images show an interior view of a king post with nearby smoke-blackened rafters supporting a tile roof (note the king post at the very top of the image) and an exterior view of several layers of timber frame supports (*courtesy of WDOAM*).

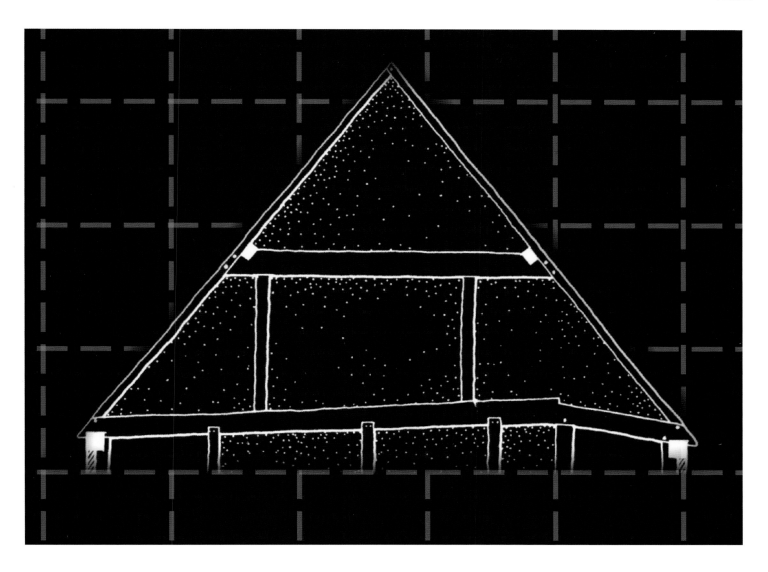

The next step in the use of timber-framed supports on the second floor is what is called queen post design. Instead of a single vertical post, there are now two with an additional cross-piece beam that provided more usable space. The diagram and the first present day image shows the gable end of the same cottage with this type of support. Notice the thatch roof. The second image, from a larger building, has an additional vertical support. Notice the brick infill in the rear wall, as well as the framing (*courtesy of WDOAM*).

Another interesting method using timber was the box-framing technique where relatively small squares, not necessarily uniform, would make up the walls of the house. Bricks could then be filled in between the timbers. Plaster covered the outside and the timbers may or may not have been covered (*permission of WDOAM*).

These two interior views of a barn built in the mid-1700s show post and tenon construction. The thatched-covered roof is supported by vertical rafters and horizontal purlins. Smaller horizontal boards connect the thatch to the supports (*permission of WDOAM*).

Two images from different interior locations show the distinctive arched braces that provide support for the timber frame. Both of these pictures are from buildings over four hundred years old (*courtesy of WDOAM*).

A present day image of timber-framed cottages in the quaint medieval-like village of Lacock, England. Observe the different types of framing.

Lavenham, England, is best known for its varied and unique buildings. Relatively recently, but sometime after WW II, somebody came up with the idea to remove the brick and plaster that covered these centuries-old houses to expose the timber frames. Now, you can walk the streets and see these distinctive and irreplaceable cottages.

Windows, like timber frames, have evolved through the years. The simplest and earliest may have been a board or animal pelt that hung over an opening. Small windows with bars would allow light in; the diamond-shaped pattern was developed because it best prevented rain from entering.

The earliest true doors were vertical boards held together by horizontal connecting boards.

These two images from a farmhouse at the Weald and Downland Open Air Museum illustrate how certain private matters were taken care of. Located on the second floor, adjacent to the bed seen in a previous image, the privy hung off the side of the house. Notice the branches that are used in the walls and ceiling and the construction of the door (*permission of WDOAM*).

Infill

Once the timber-framed structure has been erected, a house, barn, or another out-building, the subsequent issue that must be addressed is what to use to fill in the spaces between the posts. Historical experts in England refer to this as infilling. This is where the walls would be packed with material using the specialized assistance of a wallwright or dauber. In some cases a plasterer would be used to complete the walls and a thatcher used for the roof. There are numerous regional variations, but in the earliest houses the posts and beams would be left exposed. Through the centuries, as different techniques developed, walls would be constructed of a variety of materials that would hide the timber frame underneath. Yet it was still necessary to find some substance to position between the frames. The methods used in the Old Country were probably used by the colonists because they were familiar with that practice, but conditions in the New World required alternatives that offered better performance. Harsh weather conditions, including snow and severe storms (hurricanes and northeasters) necessitated that wood as shingles and clapboards be utilized to cover the cottage.

Probably the oldest and most common practice was to use what we refer to as wattle and daub. The most primitive form of this technique was to use wattle, branches from trees, to span the distance between the posts, and then add the daub. In America, a modification called "cat and daub" involved straw and clay that were molded into fairly large rolls and placed between the wooden posts. A more advanced form used in England was to position oak staves, narrow shingle-like boards, around vertical supports and then add the daub. The mud-like daub, consisting of a mixture of subsoil (clay), chopped straw, and manure, was then applied, allowed to dry, and finally coated with limewash or painted. Not suitable because of the New World's sometimes harsh environment, this English method of filling the spaces would last indefinitely if properly maintained. This technique was used until the late eighteenth century. If stone were present, thin pieces of rock would be lodged in the panels. Another method to fill the spaces was to use bricks. The first form of these lumps of clay were sun-dried in a convenient mould that could be used in the construction process. With the development of kiln-dried brick, their shape and size being more uniform, they could be used to fill the panels with distinctive patterns. But, the bricks tended to hold the dampness and were poor insulators. Wall coverings have improved in their efficiency through the recent centuries, and a variety of materials are now used to cover houses. In England, as well as in America, when renovations are done to an older home, discoveries hidden in the walls are made that sometimes show the building methods that were used hundreds of years ago. On Cape Cod and after World War II, when some of the older houses were being restored and modernized, these methods were revealed when branches were discovered in the walls.

Behind the railing leading to the second floor of this house, some of the daub has been removed to show the wattle (branches) that fills the panel (*permission of WDOAM*).

This inside view of a roof shows branches that have been woven to fill the space (*permission of WDOAM*).

Bricks in a herringbone pattern fill the walls in this building (*permission of WDOAM*).

Fireplace

A typical Cape Cod fireplace with the tools, implements, and attachments that the early occupants would have used to cook and heat the house (*courtesy of LOC*).

One of the first necessities for living in a house was to be able to build a fire for heating and cooking. For thousands of years, the hearth with the central fire provided an area for communal use that was convenient to all members of the group. This may have been why the earliest family shelters were round. As individual families built their own houses, the fire was built in the center of these structures. Without chimneys, the smoke would flow out through openings in the roof or windows on the upper story. In the oldest medieval halls, a fire was located in the central room. Vertical clay tiles were inlaid into the floor where the fire would be built. The main hall would have a table and stools for an eating and communal area; a service area at the other end of the house would allow food to be stored, prepared, and served.

A brief digression on the history of the chimney is required. Originally there was only an area where the smoke rose from the fire and exited the roof. The first actual structural chimney may have been built as early as the twelfth century in England. Additional evidence indicates that in Venice, Italy, they had been constructed as early as 1350. The wealthier the occupant, the more likely it would be for the house to have at least one chimney. The next progression regarding fire is referred to as the "smoke bay." At one end of the house a fire would be built against the wall and the smoke (hopefully) would exit through an opening in the roof. In the most primitive examples, wattle and daub would be used on the walls next to the fire. In England these types of chimneys were being used until 1621, when the danger from fires resulted in the following law, "*that no man shall elect and build up any chimney within the borough but only of brick, and to be builded above the roof of the house fower feete and a halve.*"

In America, the first recorded fire in Boston, March 16, 1634, destroyed two buildings as a result of imperfect chimneys.

Subsequently, Governor Thomas Dudley prohibited the construction of wooden chimneys and thatched roofs. Now mandated, bricks and other stones would be used to build the chimneys. With the advent of the brick fireplace and a chimney leading to and above the roof, fires could be safely contained in a restricted area. But it still didn't resolve the issue of removing the smoke and, literally, for generations, attempts were made to make a fireplace "draw" properly.

The next major step was the development of the Rumford fireplace in 1796. Tall, shallow, with angled covings and a smaller, streamlined throat in the flue, the fireplace revolutionized home heating. Homes in the city of London, England, became not only smoke-free, but also more efficient when the original fireplaces were modified.

Born in Woburn, Massachusetts, in 1765, Benjamin Thompson studied at Harvard University and spent his career involved with thermodynamics. For his work with the Bavarian Army, he was awarded the honor of Count Rumford.

Thomas Jefferson installed a Rumford fireplace at Monticello and the invention remained popular until 1850. There has been a resurgence in Rumfords and today they are being installed in new homes and homes being restored.

Designed before the Rumford fireplace, in the 1740s, a metal-lined fireplace insert known as the Franklin stove became popular by the mid-nineteenth century. Invented by Benjamin Franklin, the stove further increased the heat output and improved smoke removal. With the development of central heating, an open fire for heating was no longer required.

These two opposing views (right and bottom left) of a central hall with a fire in the center were taken at the Bayleaf Farmstead, which is located on the grounds of the Weald and Downland Open Air Museum in Singleton, England. Having no chimney, the smoke exited through an opening near the service end of the house, through the windows as seen here, or almost certainly through the openings in the roof tiles. Evidence indicates that a brick chimney was added to the house in 1636. This timber-framed house may have been built as early as 1405. In the first image, beyond the fire is one of the doors which open to the house. To the left of the door are the buttery, pantry, and service area where the food was prepared. Archival documents indicate that the table, stools, and pewter tableware used by the homeowners most likely look similar to these replicated furnishings (*permission of* WDOAM).

This is a partial view of the kitchen/pantry, which is to the left of the door seen in the preceding image (*permission of* WDOAM).

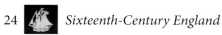

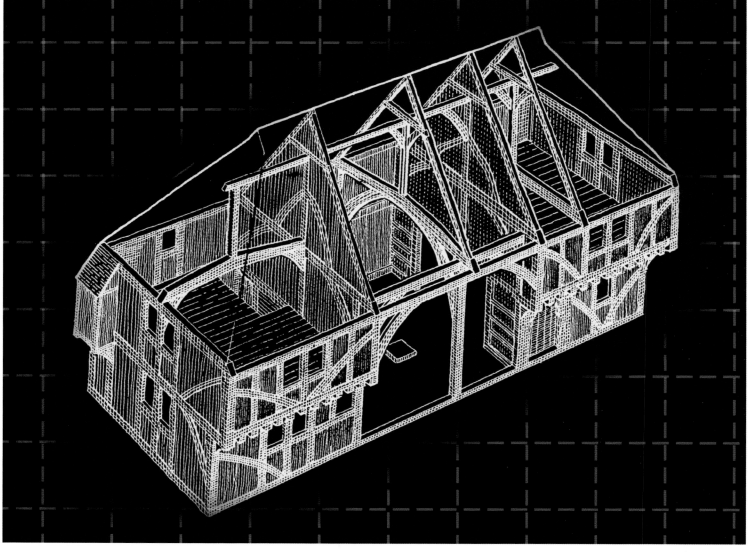

This diagram of a farmhouse illustrates several topics discussed here, including the partial use of crucks, the centrally located fire, the kitchen/pantry at the far end of the house beyond the central room, the arched brace in the bedroom on the second floor, and the privy hanging off the end of the house (*courtesy of WDOAM*).

A close-up image showing the vertical clay tiles where the fire was built on the floor in the center of the main room in this fourteenth century cottage (*permission of WDOAM*).

This primitive "smoke bay" is inside one of the cottages at the Plimoth Plantation Museum in Plymouth, Massachusetts. The soot stained wall leads to a small opening in the roof (*permission of Plimoth Plantation*).

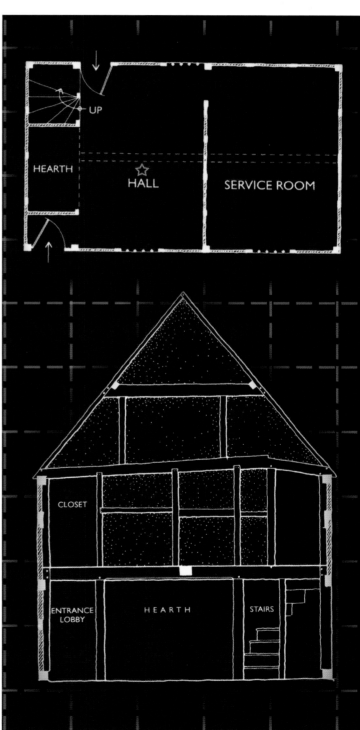

Two partitions, one on each side, and a stone-lined wall (right) make up this "smoke bay" in a house on the grounds of the Weald and Downland Open Air Museum. The house was built around 1650; a brick chimney was added in the eighteenth century. Now restored on the grounds of the museum, the house was occupied for more than three hundred years. Use the plans to locate the hearth and the type of framing (*permission of WDOAM*).

This fireplace, originally built in this house in 1609, has been restored at the Weald and Downland Museum. With sophisticated construction, there are three flues, one each for the two fireplaces on the first floor and one for the fireplace on the second floor (*permission of WDOAM*).

This fireplace and flue, found in one of the cottages at Plimoth Plantation, shows an intermediate stage with a flue, but it is not made out of brick. Unlike the Weald and Downland Museum, where all the structures are centuries old and have been restored to show their original construction, the English village at Plimoth Plantation is the best-educated evaluation of the houses the colonists built. There are no original houses remaining (*permission of Plimoth Plantation*).

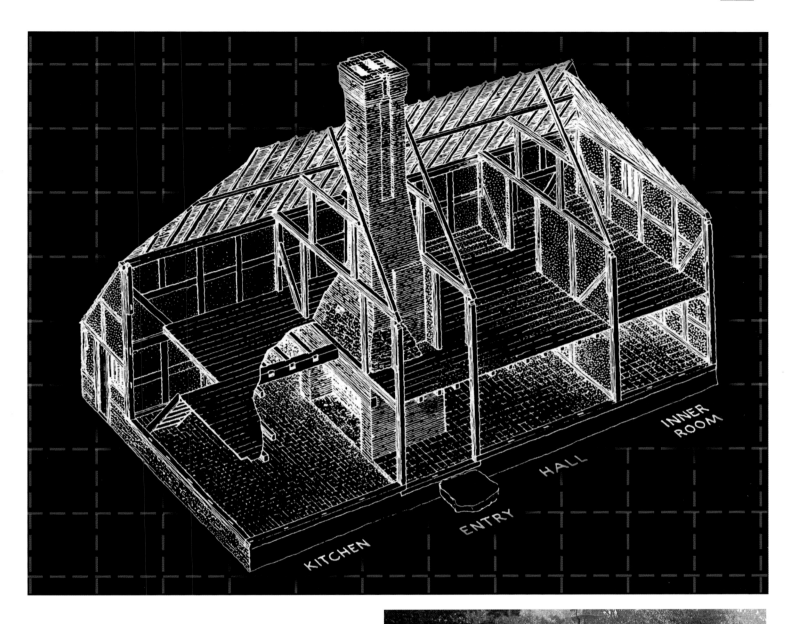

KITCHEN ENTRY HALL INNER ROOM

These three views are of the same farmhouse. More than eighty years old, the black and white image is of the house in its original location. A diagram shows the chimney design and the fireplace seen in the previous image. Smoke can be seen coming out of one of the flues in the present farmhouse on the grounds of the museum. The house has been restored to its original plan (*permission of WDOAM*).

By the nineteenth century, and seen at this house at the Weald and Downland Museum, a metal stove, with greater efficiency and increased safety, was added to the fireplace in this house (*permission of WDOAM*).

During several additions to the original house (built in the early 1700s), this new Rumford fireplace was added to what is the keeping room.

Early Seventeenth Century

1627 Plimoth Plantation

The next encounter on our journey to discover the beginnings of the Cape Cod house style is the 1627 English village at Plimoth Plantation, which is the most accurate reconstruction of the dwellings that the colonists lived in after settling in the New World. A living museum, Plimoth Plantation was started more than fifty years ago with the replica *Mayflower*, the ship that carried the Pilgrims to the New World, and the "first house," which was built on the dock near Plymouth Rock and the *Mayflower*. Now more than two miles south of the original settlement, the present day Plantation consists of not only the English Village, but also a Native American Wampanoag home site with interpreters in traditional dress, a museum with exhibits, and centers for crafts, animal husbandry, and gardening. The houses in the village are built based on the archeological record, artifacts, and accounts and articles from historical documents. In addition, houses, animal pens, fortifications with a fort and stockade fence (originally built in 1622), and other outbuildings were constructed to re-create what the English settlers built to meet their needs. One third the size of the original village, which had more houses and numerous acres of land dedicated to farming and grazing for the animals, this present day re-creation can still offer insight into the construction of what would become the Cape Cod house. From the following images, you can analyze the parameters that constitute what we consider to be this house style. Nearly square, and with a braced frame that is jointed and pegged together with stiff braces in vertical angles, a steep angle to the roof, and a covering of clapboards, these original cottages evolved into the Cape Cod house as a result of the improvement in technology and techniques in the construction methods. Tools were developed which allowed for more advancements in erecting houses that were better suited for the environment in the New World. Many of the first colonists were skilled tradesmen, including ship's carpenters familiar with construction methods. Thatch-covered roofs and "cob" walls, straw mixed with clay, may have been adequate in England, but the harsh winters in the Plimoth Colony forced the colonists to alter their house design by using different materials. The abundant forests provided a supply of wood, and running water could be harnessed to provide a variety of activities that benefitted the colonists. Considering that we may never know what these first cottages looked like, it is a safe assumption that what we see at Plimoth Plantation is the way these houses were built nearly four hundred years ago (*all photos of Plimouth Plantation used with permission of Plimouth Plantation*).

This unique chimney design was found on an old cottage in Sudbury, England.

This panorama, looking towards Plymouth Bay in the distance and taken from near the fort in the fall, is a view of the village with its different houses. Fences surround individual homes and a variety of outbuildings. Animals would have grazed in the foreground area.

Step back in time, nearly four hundred years, and view these vistas as might be seen by an individual in the mid 1620s. Looking up and down the street, interpreters in period dress act, speak, and welcome the visitor to this living museum, replicating the daily activities of that time, including cooking, gardening, animal husbandry, and blacksmithing. There is continual construction of an assortment of structures, and as can be seen in these images, a cottage. Notice the braced-framed method used in this new residence.

Compare these two sets of interior images of two relatively basic cottages. A fireplace at one end of the room, small windows with inside shutters, essential furniture brought from the Old Country, and a bed at the opposite end are the typical layout found in these 1627 cottages. Notice also that the floors in these original cottages were simply hard-packed dirt. The beds in the original cottages would also have had a canopy that protected the residents from rodent droppings from above.

A typical cottage that included a series of raised-bed vegetable gardens as seen in the foreground. Note the center chimney.

This large cottage is actually the result of an addition to an existing cottage; the section closer in this view was added after the first dwelling was constructed. Notice the two chimneys, one at each end, the supporting beams that extend through the random-width clapboards, and two doors, only one of which is visible here.

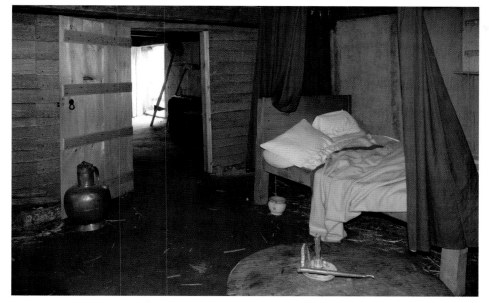

Step inside the first door and see through the opening that leads to the second half of the cottage. Notice the clapboards that were the exterior wall of the original cottage.

Stand in the doorway seen in the previous image and look into the original cottage; the door to the outside is to the right.

The sleeping area in this one cottage also includes a crib.

As cottages became larger, the area above the rafters became more important and could be used as storage, as seen here, or for additional sleeping accommodations as the families increased in size,

The windows in many of the original cottages were small and without glass; clapboards were random width and covered the exterior wall; and reeds local to the area were collected, dried, and combined to form the thatch on the roof. The harsher conditions in the New World eventually required a more permanent covering such as shingles instead of thatch.

Notice the corner where the fireplace is located, opening to a hole at the top of the wall/ceiling. There is an interior shutter which can be slid across to close the window. Tree branches were used in the rafters.

Late Seventeenth Century

Cape Cod

This book is about the architecture of a classic style dwelling that can trace its lineage in America back almost four hundred years. This book is also about history and the people who lived in these homes. It is about the farmer, yeoman, fisherman, mariner, schoolteacher, and minister, and other folks that comprised the fabric of the community. The houses identified in the following pages are also homes where, in some cases, generations of a single family lived and died. With more colonists immigrating to the New World, more than twenty thousand by 1630, these settlers extended the original settlements from the Plimoth Bay Colony and the Massachusetts Bay Colony in the Boston/Charlestown region. Houses from that area tended to be larger, with saltboxes and two-story colonials common, which are not a topic of discussion in this book. As more colonists moved south from Plimoth, it was the distinctive one-and-a-half-story house with its readily identifiable architectural style that became the homes for these farmers and fishermen. Originally part of the Plimoth Colony, Cape Cod was developed with the first community being in Sandwich in 1637. The King's Highway (now route 6A) meandered east from Sandwich along the bay side and through the villages that would become Barnstable, Yarmouth, Dennis, Brewster, and Eastham. Orleans separated in 1718 from Eastham and incorporated later in 1797. Eventually, the Outer Cape towns would become Eastham, Wellfleet, Truro, and Provincetown, which was settled last. Ride along route 6A today, follow along what was the sandy path that Timothy Dwight rode more than two centuries ago, and see numerous well-maintained Cape-style houses that are vigilant reminders of life in the eighteenth and nineteenth centuries.

The easiest answer to an inquiry about the origin of how the name of this style house came into existence nearly two centuries ago can be traced to a specific individual and a specific book. The following is an excerpt from the 1823 book *Travels in New-England and New York* by Timothy Dwight, S.T.D, LL.D., who was the former President of Yale University and wrote about his journeys throughout Cape Cod in a series of letters. He is considered to be the first to name and describe the house design and style detailed in this book.

The houses in Yarmouth are inferior to those in Barnstable, and much more generally of the class, which may be called with propriety Cape Cod houses. These have one story and four rooms on the lower floor; and are covered on the sides, as well as the roofs, with pine shingles, eighteen inches in length. The chimney is in the middle, immediately behind the front door; and on each side of the door are two windows. The roof is straight. Under it are two chambers and there are two larger and two smaller windows in the gable end. This is the general structure and appearance of the great body of houses from Yarmouth to Race Point [Provincetown]. *There are however, several varieties, but of too little importance to be described.* [Could it be that Dwight was referring to half Cape , three-quarter Capes, and full Cape houses?] *A great proportion of them are in good repair* [The same is true today]. *Generally they exhibit a tidy, neat aspect in themselves, and in their appendages, and furnish proofs of comfortable living, by which I was at once disappointed and gratified. The barns are usually neat, but always small.*

We may never know the precise houses Dwight was describing in Yarmouth, but it seems highly likely that the images of the cottages in Yarmouth found in this book may be the ones, as they are found along the side of the present day road, which was at the time the King's Highway.

That book is a precursor, by a generation, of the musings that Henry David Thoreau wrote about in *Cape Cod*, when he wandered the Cape almost forty years later. Thoreau made four trips to the Cape beginning in 1849 and stayed in several homes as he walked along the shore on his way to the tip in Provincetown. He described one house he stayed in as follows:

> We turned in land over barren hills and valleys, whither the sea, for some reason, did not follow us, and tracing up a hollow, discovered two or three sober-looking houses within a half a mile uncommonly near the eastern coast. Their garrets were apparently so full of chambers, that the roofs could hardly lie down straight, and we did not doubt there was room for us there. Houses near the sea generally low and broad. These were a story and a half high; but if you merely counted the windows in their gable ends, you would think they were many stories more or, at any rate, that the half story was the only one thought worthy of being illustrated. The great number of windows in the ends of the houses, and their irregularity in size and position, here and elsewhere on the Cape, struck us agreeably, as if each of the various occupants who had their cunabula behind had punched a hole where his necessities required it, and according to his size and stature, without regard to outside effect. There were windows for the grown folks, and Windows for the children—three of four apiece.
>
> Generally the old-fashioned and unpainted houses on the Cape looked more comfortable as well as picturesque, than the modern and more pretending ones, which were less in harmony with the scenery, and less firmly planted.

Unlike Dwight, and identifying the location of the houses he describes, the houses where Henry David Thoreau, and his traveling buddy William Ellery Channing, stayed are well documented. One, definitely in Wellfleet, and probably a second house in Eastham, are illustrated on these pages.

Another half-century later, in the early 1920s, Wallace Nutting, an author and photographer, published the book *Massachusetts Beautiful,* in which he describes and illustrates the Cape Cod cottage.

> The Cape Cod cottage has achieved the distinction of receiving this specific name. These dwellings are uniformly of one story in height although they are often erroneously called one and half stories, as they have, generally, two rooms in the attic. The eaves, however, rise directly above the first floor, as a rule, without any side wall on the second story. Further, these houses are almost always shingled. Where they are left unpainted, as is usually the case, they acquire a beautiful gray which cannot be distinguished from the stone walls found before one reaches the Cape where such house also appear.

The earliest shelters built by the colonists, probably tucked into the side of a hill, were walls made of intertwined branches with wattle and daub and a roof with a covering of thatch. Historical records indicate that numerous fires were the cause of many of these houses being destroyed. The wattle and daub in the walls was also not as effective as plank walls. A more efficient form of house construction was necessary. The first actual description of the houses that were built in Plymouth was probably from the writings of Issack de Rasieres. Seven years after the colony was founded, visiting from New

Amsterdam (New York), de Rasieres described the houses as being constructed of "hewn planks" as were the gardens surrounding the cottages, as can be seen in previous images. This has been interpreted by historians to mean that vertical boards about eight to ten inches wide were attached to the timber frame from the ground level to the roof. At a later date, clapboards and shingles would then be added to provide an outer covering. As seen in previous images, this describes the cottages at Plimoth Plantation.

Now, centuries later it is possible to accurately describe the characteristics of a Cape Cod style house. The following descriptions apply to the region around the original settlement in the Plimoth Colony and Cape Cod. These characteristics are also relevant to other areas of the country where English settlers established colonies. They, in turn, modified and adapted the house best suited for their area. For example, further south in Virginia, the front roof-line would be extended to form a porch. This was rarely found in Massachusetts, or if present, as a later addition.

What may be one of the oldest homes on Cape Cod is the Saconnesset Homestead, which was built in 1678 in West Falmouth. The original house was a full Cape with a bow roof and a chimney made of stone. Through the years, several additions and an ell have been added. Once open to the public, the house is now privately owned and maintained.

These three images, more than one hundred years old, show the homes and landscape of the Outer Cape. Top: Snow remains in this field in Eastham with a full Cape, with its short picket fence in the distance. Further along the road, barns and Greek revival houses are more common. Middle: This scene in Truro, with several easily recognizable Capes, is of one of the communities that were found throughout the town. Bottom: Also in Truro, several Capes can be seen in this geologic hollow that was created when the glacier covered and then retreated from the outer arm of the Cape about ten thousand years ago (*courtesy of EHS*).

Characteristics of the Cape Cod House

- The small, efficient Cape Cod house is rectangular in shape with the width (front) being slightly longer than the depth (side). Exceptions occur and some of the smaller cottages may reverse these proportions. When additions have been attached, the main original house is easily distinguishable.

- The earliest houses, built on sand, had no foundation and usually faced south to take advantage of the warming sun in the winter and the cooling breezes in the summer. Having no foundation, the houses, as they frequently were, could be moved to a different location. Some houses identified in this book have been moved large distances. It is well known that cottages built on Nantucket have been moved to the mainland of Cape Cod. A house in Wellfleet was originally in Plymouth, across the bay.

- Probably the most distinguishing characteristic of the Cape Cod house style is the steep gable roof. About twenty feet from soil line to peak, the side wall would have a variety of different sized windows. The second floor, with enough headroom, could provide additional bedrooms. In the oldest houses, the eaves would extend out only a few inches. The small windows with multi-panes and doors are placed directly under the eaves.

- The house was constructed of timber frames with vertical boards that were covered by clapboards on the front side. The remaining sides and the roof were covered with wood shingles.

- There was a large central chimney, which extended through the ridge line of the roof and was usually opposite the front

door. Multiple fireplaces were found in the surrounding rooms. The chimney provided structural integrity to the house, which in many cases did not have a foundation.

- There was minimal or no exterior ornamentation. The earliest homes had no fascia boards on the corners as the shingles and clapboards would butt up against each other.

All of these characteristics made these simple structures perfectly adaptable for the occupants and the surroundings where they existed.

When Dwight wrote about the variety of the Cape Cod house architectural style, he may have been referring to what we now distinguish as the three forms of the Cape Cod house. Through the years these designations have changed and we now identify the following types of Cape Cod houses based on the location of the front door and the number of windows.

These two images of two different Capes illustrate the distinction that has occurred through the centuries. From a multi-acre complex with several buildings, most of these Capes now are one- to two-acre private residences.

Top: This one-hundred-year-old postcard shows a large Cape house with open fields that was part of a farm in Wellfleet.

Bottom: Tucked behind a fence and hidden beneath the trees, this quaint three-quarter Cape remains a mystery from the road.

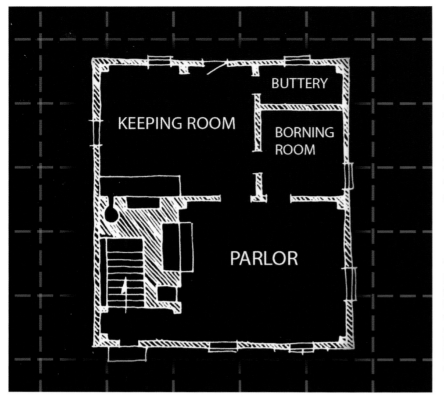

Half Cape

The half Cape, formerly known as a "house," is easily recognized with a door and the two windows to one side. It is also referred to by historians as a "three bay house:" a door and two windows. Of all the half Cape houses I found on Cape Cod, each one had a door, most commonly on the left side, and two windows side by side. Uniquely, in a village on Nantucket, I found several Capes with a door in the center and a single window on each side. These houses can be seen on page 243.

This is a first-floor plan of a half Cape and three images of this house style. There is probably no typical or standardized plan for any of these Capes, as they were built for what worked best for the occupants. The dimensions of this style are about twenty feet wide (front) by twenty-two to twenty-four feet deep (side). The interior chimney provided support for the house and, with its several fireplaces, a source of heat for the home. Notice the different locations of the chimneys (*plan courtesy of Schiffer Publishing, Ltd.*).

All beautiful and well-maintained, these three Capes show some of the possible variations that exist in these houses. Most commonly, the front door would be on the left side with the chimney directly behind it. Through the years, to add more space on the second floor, the front wall (as well as the rear wall) would be increased in height; this can be seen in the distance between the top of the windows and the roofline. Ornamentation is usually simple and basic; front doors may have pilasters and transom lights. The simplest of all Cape styles and probably the easiest to build, this may have been the first house that a family could afford and would provide shelter for a number of occupants. It was and still is easily expandable. An addition could be attached to make it a three-quarter (unlikely) or, far more likely, a full Cape. Ells could also be added to the rear of the house. Of all these different types of houses, the half Cape is the easiest to move. During modern renovations, some of the full Cape houses seen on later pages have begun life as a half Cape. When it is possible to see the frame of the house, like during reshingling, distinctive joints and different ages and types of wood are just two identifying factors that indicate the presence of an addition. Unbalanced windows and doors (not evenly spaced) and examining possible changes to interior floor plans often reveal indicators that the house has been expanded.

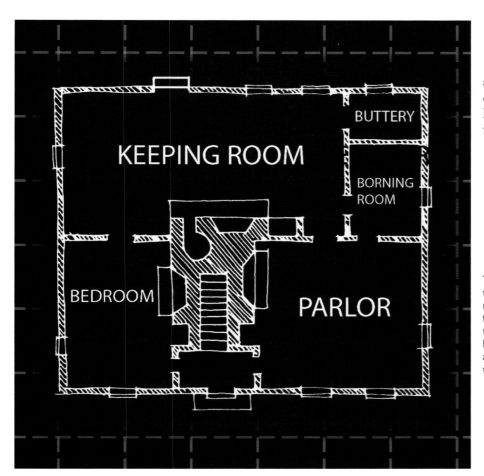

Three-Quarter Cape

The three-quarter Cape, formerly known as a "house and a half," has a door and two windows on one side and one window on the other. The house is designated as a "four bay house" with three windows and a door.

The plan and three present-day photographs show the typical three-quarter Cape, which is nearly square and measures twenty-two to maybe as much as twenty-eight feet across the front of the house. Compare this plan to the half Cape and note that the rooms are not only larger, particularly the keeping room, but also there is an additional bedroom, about half the size of the parlor, on the first floor (*plan courtesy of Schiffer Publishing, Ltd.*).

Nowadays, the larger front room may become the master bedroom and create comfortable one-floor living. Instead of expanding to make a full Cape, additions and ells, as seen in these houses, were added to the rear. The most common addition to this style house was a modern kitchen and a lavatory built behind the keeping room, which in turn became what we now think of as a family room. Notice the different location of the front door and the room behind the two front windows as being larger than the one on the other side. Several houses seen in this book have this floor plan, and the images of the different rooms in those houses make clear this living arrangement.

Full Cape

The full Cape or "double house" with a central door and two windows on each side is probably the most common and easily recognizable Cape-style house. Houses built originally as full Capes are usually recognized by a balanced symmetry with equal spacing between the windows and doors.

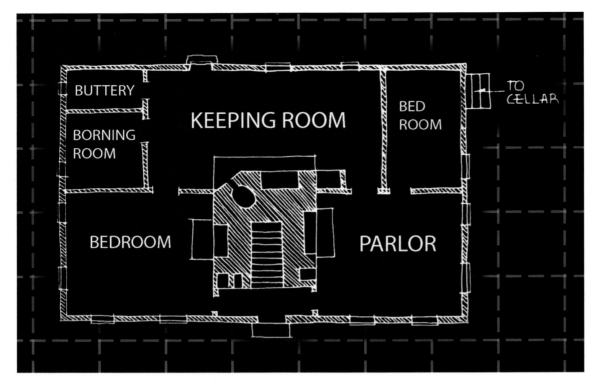

BUTTERY

BORNING ROOM

KEEPING ROOM

BED ROOM

TO CELLAR

BEDROOM

PARLOR

The most common and the largest of all Cape Cod houses is the full Cape, with a center door and two windows on each side. As large as forty feet wide, the house may have been as much as thirty feet deep. Notice on all the floor plans that the front rooms all had fireplaces with or without mantels.

In the photographs, the three houses are easily recognizable as this architectural style but still exhibit a variety of construction detail. Early houses, the owners not wanting to appear ostentatious, would have basic trim and fixtures. The picket fence is still found in front of many of these houses. Outbuildings and additions were also found on these properties.

So what is this? Maybe a missing link? It seems to be a three-quarter Cape, but all the windows are on the one side of the door; a knee wall on the second floor provides additional height for upstairs bedrooms. Also, notice the hints of Greek revival trim. Like the old days, there are clapboards on the front wall with shingles on the other walls and roof (courtesy of EHS).

The designated rooms in all Capes had the same basic function, and as the houses became larger, the rooms not only increased in size, but there were more of them. Some of the rooms and their uses are obvious, others not so. The most important room in the house was probably the keeping room, which we would now consider to be the kitchen. It had the largest fireplace and an additional beehive oven for cooking. The keeping room served many functions for the family; it was a place to eat, meet, do chores, and a play room for the kids. Located off the keeping room, there would be two additional smaller, but still important, rooms. The first was the buttery, similar to a pantry, where food was prepared and kitchen items stored. Beneath the buttery was a cellar, where food could be kept cool in the summer and stored in the winter. In some photos in this book, a small "doghouse" can be seen on the side of the house that leads to this cellar. The second important room was the borning room and, as the name implies, this is where the babies were born. It may have also been used as a bedroom for younger members of the family. Being near the keeping room, it was a warm room and also may not have had any windows, which eliminated any drafts. This room also served as a temporary resting place for the recently deceased before they were moved to the parlor for a minister's visit and a possible ceremony. An outside privy would be near the house. Several of the homes seen in these pages didn't have modern plumbing until the mid-1900s. During renovation and remodeling, one of these two rooms would become a lavatory, the other a modern pantry, or den/office. The parlor, usually on the southeast corner of the house, warmed by the sun, was the finest room in the house, with finished paneled walls, wainscoting, a cupboard with quality glassware and wine for special visits, and fine furniture. Minister's visits, weddings, and funerals were some of the special events that took place here. The second floor, depending on the size of the house, would have a variety of bedrooms and closets tucked under the eaves. As you follow along and visit the interior of numerous homes in this book, it is possible to see the diversity and range of variations that exist. Each in their own way has made the living conditions for the occupants more comfortable.

Dating Houses

While it is not the intent of this book to determine the age of, or year of construction of any house identified in these pages, a brief discussion may be helpful to put in perspective some of the interesting stories associated with some of these properties. Many Cape Cod houses, as well as other houses in Southeastern Massachusetts, are identified not only by the obvious street number, but also by a plaque or sign with a date that indicates when the property was constructed. Many of these dates, like the nearby soil, can be taken with a grain of sand. In October of 1827, there was a significant fire at the Barnstable County Courthouse that destroyed most of the records, including deeds and supporting documents. Only one volume, basically the year 1806, was saved. A number of documents prior to 1827 were collected and re-created from families and attorneys' records. Unfortunately, many details for numerous other properties across the Cape were not made available, and any possible records do not survive.

A more rigorous examination of the property may require more expertise, but it is possible to examine some characteristics that offer the enthusiast the possibility of dating or determining the history of an old house. The internal timber framework, many times not visible (maybe you can get into the attic or cellar), offer clues to whether the house was built as a smaller house and then later enlarged. Covered by shingles and clapboards, it is difficult to tell from the outside, but inside, are all the boards uniform? Do they join in such a way to indicate that they had been originally built together? Look for adze marks on beams that point toward the conclusion that they may have been reassembled. If it is possible, look for saw marks. The oldest type of sawing was called "pit sawing" and left almost vertical lines on the wood. Pit sawing was no longer used after 1800. Look for anomalies, differences that suggest changes have been made. Through the years these houses have been repaired, restored, and modernized with room changes, yet with close observation it is possible to see some of the not-so-obvious improvements or changes made to the fabric of the building.

Compare this eighty-year-old photograph of an attic in a house in Truro, which no longer exists, with not only other houses found throughout the book but also with buildings from the Weald and Downland Museum in England. Several interesting characteristics include the wide roof boards, the peg holding the joint together, and the marks on the connecting beams that very probably indicate that at one time the boards had been taken apart and then reconnected (*courtesy of LOC*).

Pit sawing, as seen in this archival image, involved a trench with two men sawing timbers from a tree trunk. Distinctive vertical marks on the timbers can be used to indicate the use of this type of saw, which was no longer operated after about 1800. Rotary saws then became popular and their resulting marks were/are characteristically different. Pit sawing produced angled straight lines; rotary saw marks were circular.

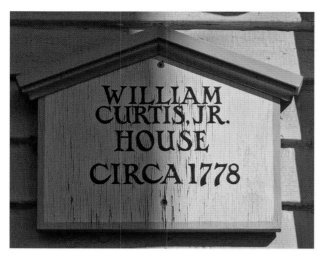

Many old Cape houses will have signs on the front wall that indicate the year of construction. Some will also mention the local historical society, lending more credence to the date the house was built. Many houses, especially in the quiet villages of Southeastern Massachusetts and Cape Cod, have a long history in their location, and numerous records substantiate the date on the sign.

Usually located near the trim board on the front wall of the house, and about half way up, this metal plaque, provided by the U.S. Department of the Interior, indicates that this property has been examined, researched in local and state documents, and undergone extensive scrutiny to determine its age and date of construction. Numerous documents are created that attest to the date and substantiate the claim. Not only time consuming, this process can also be very expensive.

Windows are a good indicator of the age of the house. The earliest, as seen in the Peak House, are small diamond shaped pieces of glass grouped together to form a window. These were in common use until the 1720s, when glass then became available in larger sizes. The first windows were strictly utilitarian in terms of location and size, but by the end of the century, symmetrical facades with consistent window design were the rule. Large two-story colonials may have had twelve over twelve lights (panes) or possible twelve over eight. The smaller Cape, in the eighteenth century, usually had windows featuring nine over nine or nine over six lights. Later in the century, six over six lights became common. Until the mid 1800s, the upper sash was fixed and the lower sash, when open, had to be either pegged or braced open. By the nineteenth century and larger glass sizes, windows were made with two over two lights or even one over one.

In addition to the windows, doors can also be used to help date a house. The earliest and, previously discussed, are the batten doors made of vertical planks held together by horizontal braces. Through the years, and with usual maintenance, many of these doors have been replaced. Hardware found on doors and throughout the house is also a measure of the antiquity of the property. The earliest hardware was wrought iron and made by the local blacksmith. Strap hinges, used on doors, were made in England until about the 1830s.

Determining the age of a house, especially if it is yours, is a fascinating and interesting exploration. Other avenues of investigation that should be considered in establishing the age of a house should include the type of nails that are used in the construction, the nature of the paint found throughout the house, the material used to make the walls, the form of the fireplace and chimney, and an evaluation of the size and style of moldings. With more study, there are other additional avenues that can be utilized to hopefully find the answer.

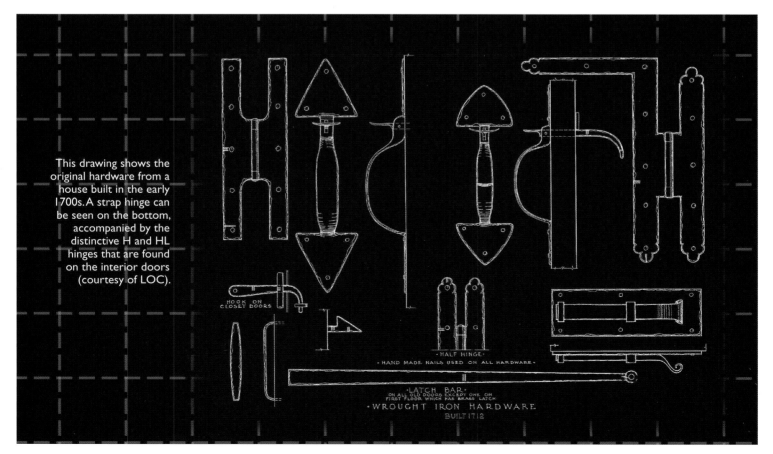

This drawing shows the original hardware from a house built in the early 1700s. A strap hinge can be seen on the bottom, accompanied by the distinctive H and HL hinges that are found on the interior doors (courtesy of LOC).

Historic Homes

Thomas Prence House, 1646
Eastham, Massachusetts

The Governor Thomas Prence House, its history well documented, was built in Eastham in 1646. A nearby fort on a hill overlooking Nauset Marsh was built in 1644. Born in England about 1600, Thomas Prence arrived in Plymouth on November 9, 1621, on the ship *Fortune*, the first ship to follow the *Mayflower* to the New World. He first resided in what is now Duxbury, and later moved and co-founded the town of Eastham on Cape Cod. First settled by the Nauset tribe of Native Americans, Eastham was not colonized by Europeans until 1644. Thomas Prence was an important local political figure. He was elected, beginning in 1633, as the fourth, eighth, and twelfth Governor of the Plymouth Bay Colony. The Prence house was built on a piece of land less than fifty yards from a salt water creek and about a half mile from the Atlantic Ocean, near what is now known as Nauset Beach. The exact location of the house at the present time is unknown, but was in the general area of what is now the Eastham Information Booth. This simple half Cape was home to Thomas, probably his second wife Mary Collier (1635), and his children, of which there may have been as many as nine. Left with four children when his first wife died, before he settled in Eastham, Thomas and Mary had five more offspring who lived in this house.

This structure no longer exists; the house was taken down sometime after this image was captured, which was before 1880 according to the Library of Congress. The Governor Prence House with the accompanying photograph and plans offers us an opportunity to examine and infer some of the characteristics of one of the earliest Capes that were built outside of the Plymouth Bay Colony. At the time of this photograph, the "three bay," two windows and a door, half Cape was used as a barn for sheep. The chimney had been removed, but the distinguishing features are easily discernible. The dwelling faced south, the steep roofline extended to the top of the windows and the door, the front wall is clapboarded, with shingles covering the other walls, and the structure is nearly square. The original front door step is now on display at the Pilgrim Monument in Provincetown (*courtesy of LOC*).

SOUTH ELEVATION

EAST ELEVATION

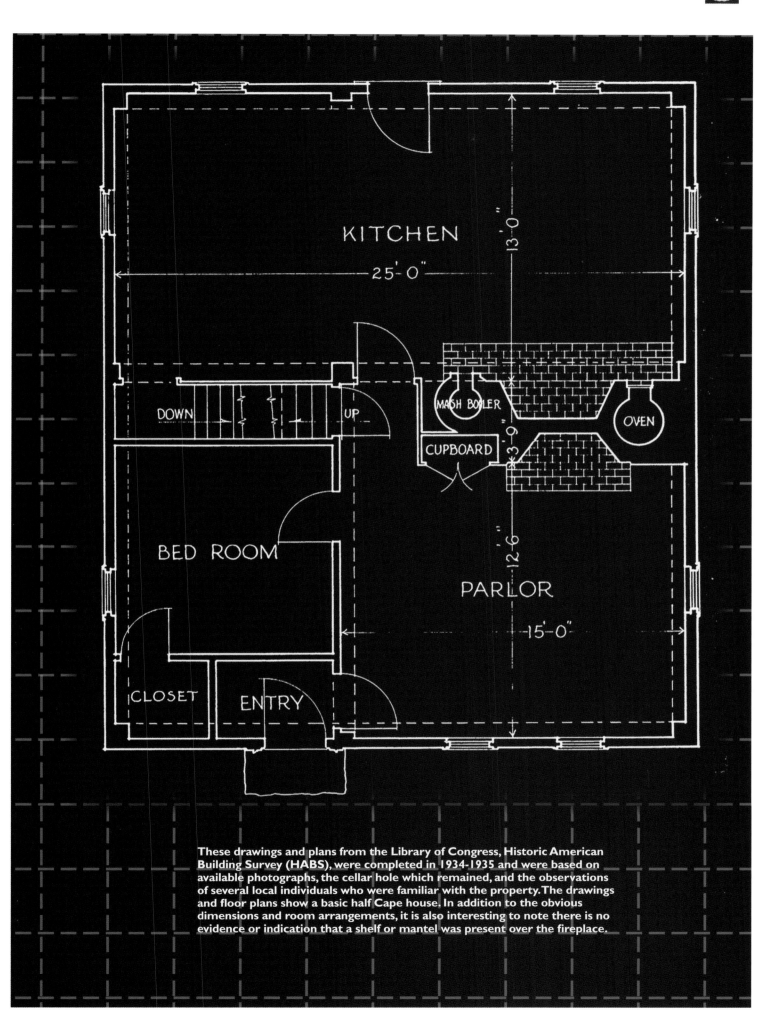

KITCHEN

13'-0"

25'-0"

DOWN   UP

MASH BOILER   OVEN

CUPBOARD

3'-9"

BED ROOM

12'-6"

PARLOR

15'-0"

CLOSET   ENTRY

These drawings and plans from the Library of Congress, Historic American Building Survey (HABS), were completed in 1934-1935 and were based on available photographs, the cellar hole which remained, and the observations of several local individuals who were familiar with the property. The drawings and floor plans show a basic half Cape house. In addition to the obvious dimensions and room arrangements, it is also interesting to note there is no evidence or indication that a shelf or mantel was present over the fireplace.

Peak House, 1680
Medfield, Massachusetts

The Peak House in Medfield, Massachusetts, is one of the earliest seventeenth century houses in the United States that is still standing and preserved. Originally built in 1650, the house was destroyed by fire in 1676 during King Philip's War with the Native Americans. In addition, more than 30 houses, several barns, and two mills in Medfield were razed by more than 1000 Indians who raided the town during the war. The house was rebuilt about 1680, and the original owners, Benjamin and Dorcas Clark, with their nine children, called this home. About fourteen feet by twenty six feet and with a footprint of fewer than four hundred square feet, the three levels allowed significant living space. Not challenged by the weather conditions that houses on the Cape had to contend with, the Peak House was able to have the two additional stories. In 1924, the house was deeded to the Medfield Historical Society by its then owners, and a total restoration was undertaken. Now on the U.S. National Register of Historic Places, the Peak House at 347 Main Street is open to the public during the summer.

A sign in front of the house describes some of the history of the dwelling.

A present-day view of the house.

This 1934 black and white image and the following three plans were recorded as part of the Library of Congress' Historic American Building Survey (HABS) (*Courtesy of LOC*).

Glass for windows in early houses was limited—small sizes were used to produce this diamond shaped pattern.

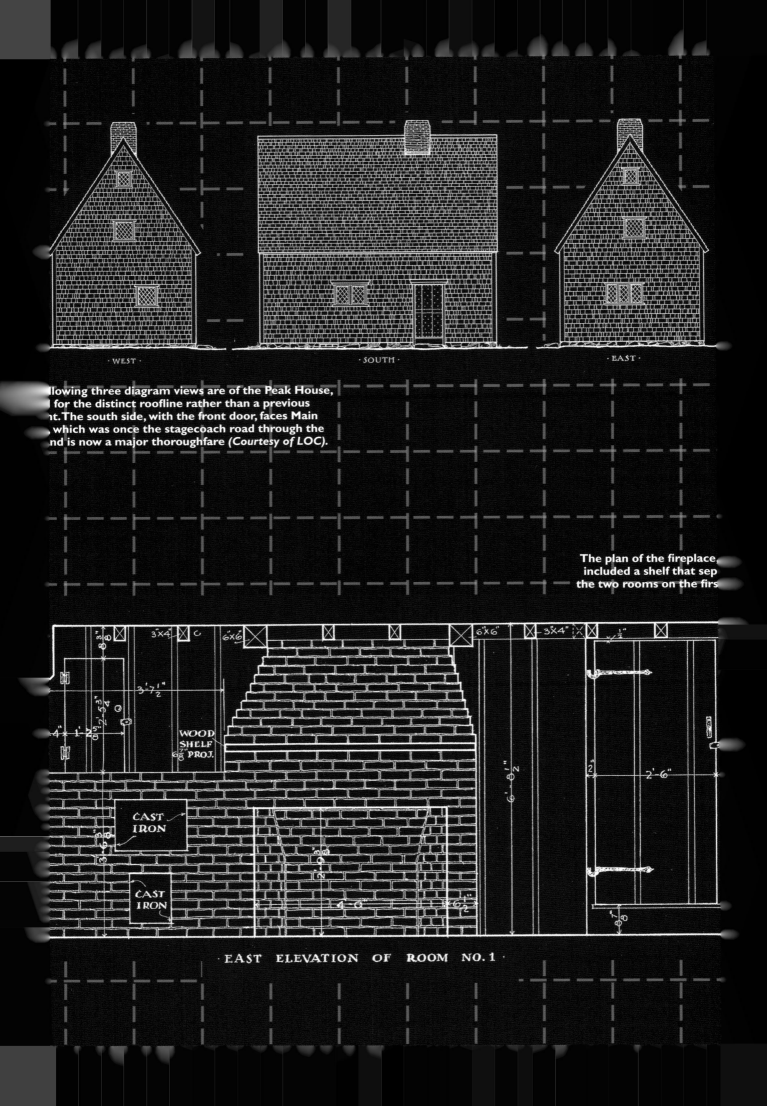

·WEST· ·SOUTH· ·EAST·

llowing three diagram views are of the Peak House,
 for the distinct roofline rather than a previous
nt. The south side, with the front door, faces Main
 which was once the stagecoach road through the
nd is now a major thoroughfare *(Courtesy of LOC)*.

The plan of the fireplace,
included a shelf that sep
the two rooms on the firs

3"x4" 6"x6" 6"x6" 3"x4"

WOOD
SHELF
6⅞" PROJ.

CAST
IRON

CAST
IRON

2'-6"

· EAST ELEVATION OF ROOM NO. 1 ·

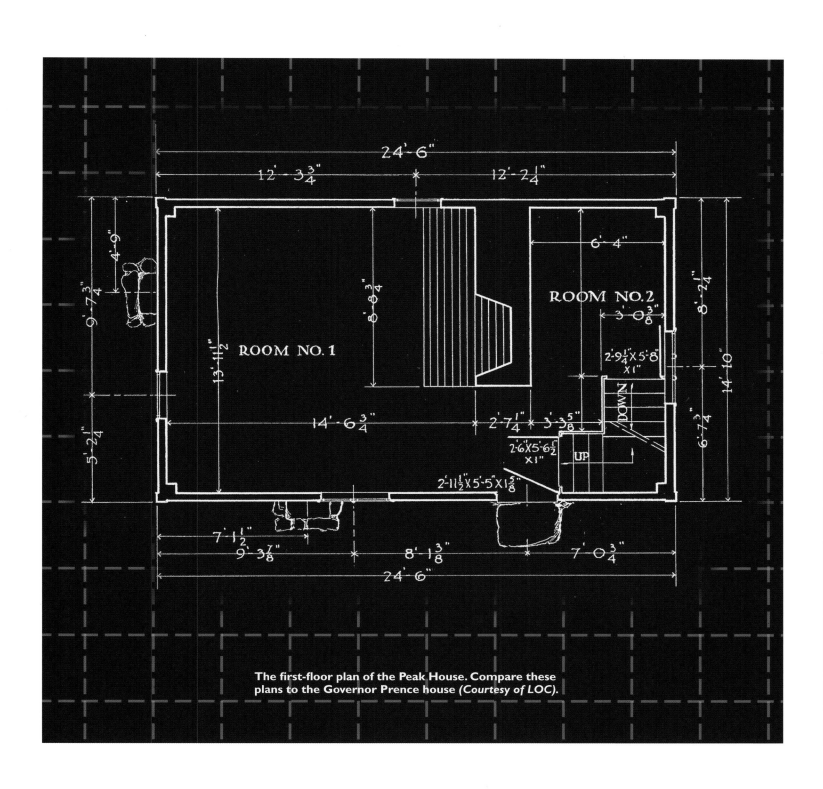

The first-floor plan of the Peak House. Compare these plans to the Governor Prence house *(Courtesy of LOC).*

Knowles Doane House, 1765
Eastham, Massachusetts

Although numerous Capes have been repaired, renovated, restored, and modernized, this traditional "half house" has retained its fabric and style after more than two hundred and forty-five years. Near what was once the center of the town of Eastham, this house was built by a member of the Doane family, who were part of the original settlers in 1644. Facing west, this is just one of several older homes in the area. Owned subsequently by one other family for more than one hundred years, it wasn't until the 1930s, during major renovations, that electricity and plumbing were added to the house. At that time, the barn was sold and rolled down a nearby road, becoming part of a different property. An addition was added to the rear of the house, which included a modern kitchen, bedroom, and a garage under the house. The windows in the earliest part of the house are original. More than fifty years ago, a new furnace was installed, insulation added, and the chimneys and flues restored with the original bricks that had been made by the Barnstable Brick Co. Although suitable for year-round living, the house is now used primarily as a summer residence.

Two views of the house, which sits close to the road, with the addition to the rear. The side of the house faces south.

A view out of one of the original front windows, with the typical nine over six panes, and with the street and a barn in the background.

Two opposite views of the front door, *(above and opposite, top)* with four panes of glass above to allow light to enter the hallway, basic trim on the outside with strap hinges on the outer door, an inner Christian door with paneling in the shape of a cross that indicated the occupants tithed the church, and a V in the wood on the floor that drained water. The cork would be removed in a "southwester" to allow water to escape. Also, notice the wide floor boards, which are original.

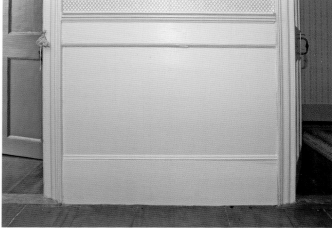

At twenty-four inches, this panel in the parlor is highly unusual; it was illegal to use lumber this size in homes as the king had rights to these large trees for use in his ships. The front door is to the left and the original bedroom is to the right.

A door opens to the bedroom just off the parlor. Notice the sign on the wall, which is also found in a previous image.

The fireplace in the parlor is typical, with little ornamentation. The book shelves to the left of the fireplace would originally have had glass doors, some fancy wine glasses, and a bottle of wine for the local reverend when he visited. Hence, it was frequently called a "minister cabinet."

This is a view of the fireplace in the keeping room, which was recently rebuilt. The functional beehive oven is to the left. To use the oven, a vigorous fire would be made for four or five hours in the fireplace (to heat the bricks). Flour would be sprinkled on the oven floor and if it turned brown, the oven was ready. The flue and damper would be closed and the coals raked out and moved to the fireplace. Usually, it was possible to have four bakings before the oven cooled. The door to the right of the fireplace now leads to a closet, but originally led to a root cellar. The window to the left can be seen in the south view of the house.

The borning room was located off the keeping room. This room was also used for a place to put the recently departed on view before burial.

A close-up view of the beehive oven, which had its own separate flue.

A view of the keeping room with the front parlor through the opening to the right. Find the windows to the left in the exterior image of this side of the house.

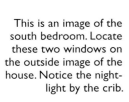

With the front door to the left, the "Paul Revere" stairs lead to two bedrooms on the second floor. The railing at the top of the stairs is removable to allow furniture to be moved into the rooms.

This is an image of the south bedroom. Locate these two windows on the outside image of the house. Notice the night-light by the crib.

An old three-board closet door in the bedroom.

Probably older than the actual house itself is this door with four window panes. Opening into the second bedroom, the door may have originally been on a ship, but has definitely been recycled from a previous structure. The thumb latch is handmade, as are the nails that hold the door together.

A small, classic fireplace in the bedroom. The two-board door on the left leads to the other bedroom. Notice the night-light.

Timothy Mayo House
Eighteenth Century
Eastham, Massachusetts

Local records indicate that a small half house may have been built here as early as 1720. The three-quarter house shown in detail here was constructed ten to twenty years later. Exceptionally well preserved, this house, typical of eighteenth century construction in Eastham, has sparse detailing with narrow eaves and end boards. Several additions and changes in windows indicate various stages of construction. In the late 1700s, there was a small hamlet in this area near the King's Highway that included a windmill. On what was once probably a thirty-acre farm, this bow- roofed Cape still has fruit trees growing on the property.

Compare the present-day image of the house with one taken in the late 1800s. A vent pipe for modern plumbing is the only difference. The addition to the rear now has a modern kitchen that was built using boards and beams retrieved from a barn that was dismantled from the property (*black and white courtesy of EHS*).

The east side of the house, which may be the oldest. The chimney and fireplace in the small extension of the wall were added later.

The rear of the house showing the various additions. The white door at the corner of the modern kitchen extension and the old house leads to the brick root cellar.

The rear roofline shows a slight bow.

The west side of the house with the kitchen to the rear and a small ell off that.

This small window, although obviously a modern addition, is found in the oldest part of the house. It is on the opposite wall to the window shown earlier in the east side view.

Looking from the keeping room, wide-plank floors lead to the front door.

This bedroom with a fireplace and cupboard is found to the right of the front door.

The keeping room fireplace—the previous bedroom is through the door to the left.

Narrow stairs, typical of older houses, lead to the second floor.

A small, brick root cellar also contains the pump that provides water to the house.

A small room in the attic showing the peg and tenon construction.

Construction details seen in the inside roof.

This second-floor bedroom window can be seen in the east side view.

Jonathan Kendrick House, 1792
South Orleans, Massachusetts

Considered to be a classic, full-colonial Cape, this is the only house in the town of Orleans, Massachusetts, that was part of the HABS survey in 1934. It was built in 1792 by Captain Jonathan Kendrick (1761-1839), a cousin of Captain John Kendrick (1740-1793), who lived in nearby Wareham, Massachusetts, and was in command of the *Columbia,* the first U.S. vessel to sail west around Cape Horn, thus opening the Northwest fur trade.

Taken more than seventy years apart, these two images show the Captain Kendrick House practically unchanged. With the trees grown, the house blends beautifully into its setting.

These two views show the front of the house; compare these to the previous plans. Whether in the middle of the summer, or during a snowstorm, the Captain Kendrick house, more than two hundred years old, gives the impression that it fits into its surroundings.

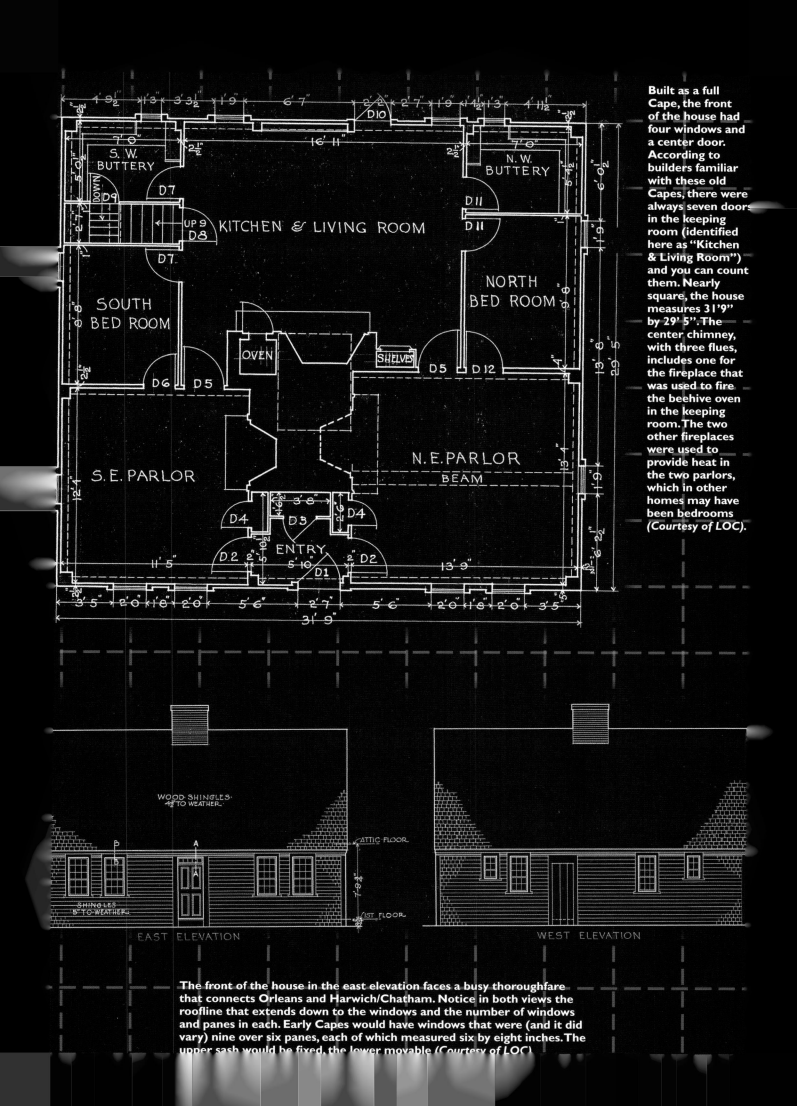

S. W. BUTTERY

KITCHEN & LIVING ROOM

N. W. BUTTERY

SOUTH BED ROOM

NORTH BED ROOM

OVEN

SHELVES

S. E. PARLOR

N. E. PARLOR

BEAM

ENTRY

DOWN
UP 9

16' 11"

31' 9"

29' 5"

D1 D2 D3 D4 D5 D6 D7 D8 D9 D10 D11 D12

EAST ELEVATION

WEST ELEVATION

WOOD SHINGLES 4½" TO WEATHER

ATTIC FLOOR

SHINGLES 5" TO WEATHERS

1ST FLOOR

Built as a full Cape, the front of the house had four windows and a center door. According to builders familiar with these old Capes, there were always seven doors in the keeping room (identified here as "Kitchen & Living Room") and you can count them. Nearly square, the house measures 31'9" by 29' 5". The center chimney, with three flues, includes one for the fireplace that was used to fire the beehive oven in the keeping room. The two other fireplaces were used to provide heat in the two parlors, which in other homes may have been bedrooms *(Courtesy of LOC).*

The front of the house in the east elevation faces a busy thoroughfare that connects Orleans and Harwich/Chatham. Notice in both views the roofline that extends down to the windows and the number of windows and panes in each. Early Capes would have windows that were (and it did vary) nine over six panes, each of which measured six by eight inches. The upper sash would be fixed, the lower movable *(Courtesy of LOC).*

Rowell House
Eighteenth Century
Wellfleet, Massachusetts

When the Cape Cod National Seashore (CCNS) was proposed (late 1950s/early 1960s), HABS arranged with architects and historians to survey houses and other buildings to determine their age and significance. This half house was identified as the oldest home on the Lower Cape. In 1827, a fire in the Barnstable County Courthouse destroyed many records, so it is not possible to ascertain the exact date of construction. Oral history from a previous owner dates the house to about 1730, and according to the HABS architect, it appears to have been built mid-eighteenth century. Very little information remains regarding the early years of the house. As with many of the other early houses built on this outer arm of the Cape, this house faces south and is in the lee of a hill. Now surrounded by trees, two hundred years ago this area would have been treeless and only about a mile from the Atlantic Ocean. Unlike other Capes of that era, which were built rectangular with no side additions, this one was erected with a five-foot wing to the left of the house. Also unlike many other Capes, there have been no additions. Study the images and plans, completed more than fifty years ago, of this very old half Cape. The house measures 26'6" by 27' with vertical planks on a heavy timber frame and simple exterior trim. Notice the variety of windows on the sides of the house and the different number of panes in various windows. The interior trim is mitered and indicative of mid-eighteenth century construction techniques. Near a pond, the house is at the end of a clam shell driveway.

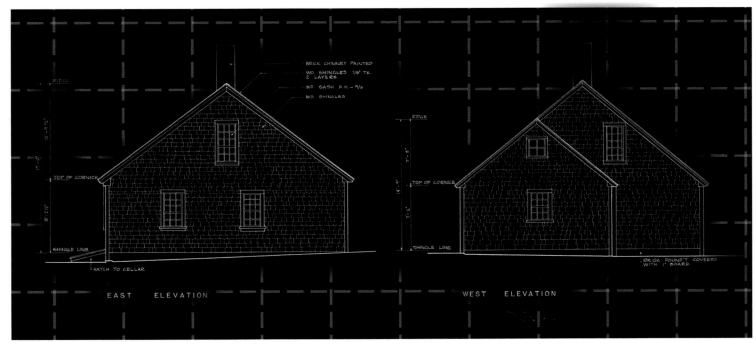

EAST ELEVATION   WEST ELEVATION

(plan and images courtesy of LOC)

Captain John Hawes, 1736
Chatham, Massachusetts

Fortuitously, while looking for another house to photograph, I came across this old Cape located on a busy thoroughfare in Chatham, Massachusetts. Well preserved and in excellent condition, the Captain John Hawes House is remarkable in that it is still standing, as it's found in a commercial area with several busy shopping centers nearby. Authorities and historians have suggested that the dwelling is nearly ninety-five percent original. The house is also unoccupied, which gives us the opportunity to examine the interior in more detail. Facing north, the property is located on the south side of the main road between Chatham and Harwich. Although the house may look like a traditional full Cape, with a pair of windows on each side of the door, closer examination reveals the offset (to the right/west) chimney and front door, which probably indicates that at one time this house was a half Cape. The front door with pilasters has a four-light transom. The windows, with typical nine over six panes, are in projecting frames that probably indicate plank construction in the walls. Note the windows directly below the roof-line. A sea captain, John Hawes, built this house in 1736, when he married Abigail Doane of Eastham. Hawes family records, since the houses passed from father to son, trace the ownership and give details regarding the property. Samuel, the grandson, was the owner of record in 1858, and the house can be identified on a local map of the area. Another unique connection to this house is that several Doane houses in Eastham are identified elsewhere in these pages. It wasn't until after 1950 that electricity and plumbing were added to the house. Recently sold, the house was an antique store for more than twenty years. There was also a blacksmith shop in a recently built barn behind the house.

A view of the east side of the house with the unusual asymmetrical window arrangement. The two windows at the top are in a bedroom—the variety of doors can also be seen here. Note the lean-to which extends the house near the back door.

The southwest corner of the Cape, with the lean-to that only extends across part of the back. It is possible to identify some of these windows from the interior views.

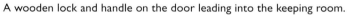

Inside the lean-to, before going into the keeping room, this post and beam have been marked with numerals to indicate how they were, and are presently, connected. It is difficult to see their length, but note the thickness and width of the roof boards which are just above the joint.

A wooden lock and handle on the door leading into the keeping room.

Two opposite images of the keeping room. The east-facing photograph shows the backdoor entrance, a pantry that was converted to a bathroom, another room that was converted into a kitchen, and the door that would have led to a bedroom. The west-facing photograph shows the fireplace (without a beehive oven), a door leading to the parlor, a bedroom, a door (and behind it, stairs leading to the second floor), a present day pantry, and a gray door that leads to the cellar. Identify the windows from the outside as they relate to these interior rooms.

A narrow closet to the left of the fireplace and the parlor in the background.

Two views of the parlor with its hand- painted walls. Notice the boards on the lower part of the wall, which are full length but not as wide as those in the Knowles Doane house. The opening to the far left of the fireplace leads to the hallway and front door.

An image of the front, east room with its own fireplace. The open closet here is also the same as the one in the parlor. The front door and part of a transom light can be seen through the opening.

Painted stairs lead to the second floor. Narrow and steep, there is no handrail until you get to the top.

A close-up of a peg holding a cross-beam together on the second floor.

There are two bedrooms on the second floor; this is the one facing west.

This wood door leads to the second bedroom.

Three distinctively different "doors" can be found in the upstairs east bedroom: a two-board door opens into a bathroom, the middle door opens into a closet, and the door on the right is seen in a previous image.

A view of the closets and beams in the east bedroom.

Swift-Daley House, 1741
Eastham, Massachusetts

Several of the houses described and illustrated in this book are open to the public during the tourist season. Many also include a variety of furnishings from eras past. The Swift-Daley House on busy Route 6 in Eastham is open during the summer season, and docents from the Eastham Historical Society provide perspective about the property. Characteristics of the Cape Cod house exhibited in these images are the nearly symmetrical shape, low first-floor height, closely fit openings with a steep gabled roof, and a center chimney. The original owner, Joshua Knowles, had this house and property that extended to the east as far as Nauset Marsh (about a 1/4 mile away). The owners through the years are well documented, and a history of the house and the outbuildings is almost fully known. One particular resident family that is of historical significance is Nathaniel and Gustavus Swift, who owned the house in the mid-nineteenth century. A butcher by trade, Gustavus revolutionized the meat market. Beginning in 1860, with a single steer he butchered, Swift sold the meat locally as he travelled the roads on a wagon. By 1885, Gustavus had moved closer to a source of cattle, first Albany, then Buffalo, and finally to Chicago, where he incorporated his business as we now know it today, Swift & Company. Successive owners may not have had the same notoriety, but the property, now maintained by the Eastham Historical Society, is in excellent condition even after two hundred and fifty years.

Two older images of the Swift-Daley house, both undated, that demonstrate the simplicity and beauty, in whatever season, of the Cape Cod house style (*images courtesy of EHS*).

The house faces east to what was probably the Old King's Highway; this view is of the south side. The front was recently re-shingled.

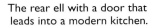

The rear ell with a door that leads into a modern kitchen.

Three views of the keeping room. Narrow back stairs, located between a pantry to the left and a bedroom to the right, lead to the second floor. On the right are two rooms: one would have been a borning room and the other a buttery. The fireplace also has a beehive oven for baking.

One of the rooms on the south side of the keeping room.

There are two rooms in the front of the house; on the south side is a parlor, shown in these two images, and on the north side is a bedroom. These two views were shot in opposite directions; the fireplace is on the inside wall. To the right of the basic cupboard is a hallway with stairs to the left, front door to the right, and the bedroom beyond,

Two opposite views of the front downstairs bedroom.

Angled stairs lead to the second floor. Similar stairs can be seen in two of the Doane houses.

Two bedrooms are located on the south side of the second floor. Compare the windows to the outside view of the south side to determine their location.

Samuel B. Dottridge House, 1808
Cotuit, Massachusetts

This quaint full Cape on Main Street, Cotuit began as a half Cape more than thirty miles away in Harwich (which included present day Brewster). Originally constructed about 1790, the house consisted of a bedroom/parlor in the front and a keeping room in the rear. Born in 1786 near the Tower of London in England, Samuel B Dottridge immigrated to America and trained as a cabinet maker in Brewster. The owner of the house was the widow Abigail Chase, who married Samuel B. Dottridge about 1807. In 1811, with a team of oxen, this house was dragged east along the King's Highway from Brewster to the western side of Barnstable and then south to Cotuit on the shore of the bay. Fishing, salt works, and farming were the principal activities in Cotuit. Dottridge, who was a Quaker, used to walk to church in Barnstable every Sunday. He did so barefoot so he wouldn't wear out his shoes. His wife Abigail died in 1848 at the age of 71. Samuel remarried, moved to Sandwich, and died in 1855. The original homestead in Cotuit remained in the Dottridge family until it became the home of the Santuit-Cotuit Historical Society. It is now open to the public for visits during the summer season and for special events throughout the year.

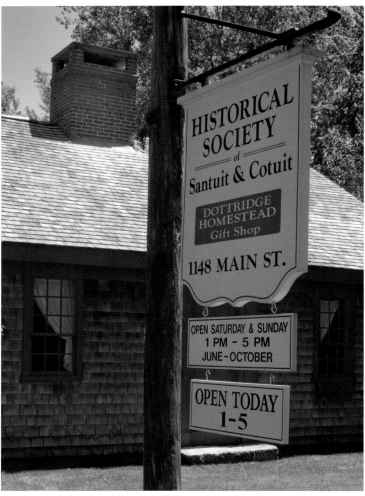

Now a museum and owned by the Santuit and Cotuit Historical Society, the Samuel B. Dottridge Homestead is open to the public from June to October, as well as for special society events. A full Cape, there is also a barn in the back that houses additional local exhibits.

A lilac bush, prized by early settlers, stands at the corner of the house; the windows are to the parlor. Notice the nine over six panes in the window and the sparse trim. Unlike other Capes, this does not have clapboards on the front wall.

The basic front door, with limited decoration and a four light transom, not only provides an address and the age of the house, but a plaque dedicated to the previous owners who donated the house.

Compare the two sides of the house with the number and arrangement of windows. The second floor of the house is not open to the public.

Notice the lack of detail in these three views of the rear of the house. The two-board batten door with strap hinges is a characteristic of these early Capes.

Three views of the keeping room. As a museum, many period pieces are on display. Notice the beamed ceiling and the doors that lead to a parlor and a bedroom in the front of the house.

Two images taken in the parlor show the beautifully painted floor, a basic cupboard, a fireplace, which is one of three on the central chimney, and period furniture. To the left of the cupboard is the front door, stairs that lead to the second floor, and the bedroom beyond.

Across the street and behind a rose-covered fence sits a later vintage and
larger Cape. The smaller chimney probably signifies central heating.

Atwood-Higgins House, 1730
Wellfleet, Massachusetts

Lost in antiquity, there may have been a primitive house on this location as early as 1635, nine years before Eastham (which included present day Wellfleet) was settled. Refer to the Prence house discussed earlier. But it is well known that the full Cape you see here started out as a half Cape more than three hundred years ago. Tracing history and dating houses is difficult. However, historians and architects identify this home and the Rowell House (page 68) mentioned earlier, as two of the most archaic houses on the Outer Cape. The previous owner and an ancestor of the original owner, George Higgins, had been in the process of restoring the property to its original condition from 1919 until he passed away. Thomas Atwood purchased the property for less than four hundred dollars in 1805 and was the second great-grandfather of George Higgins, who subsequently inherited the house. The original half Cape was 21' wide by 27' deep; when expanded, the full Cape was 35' wide. An 8' by 14' ell was also added, which included a bedroom and a west buttery. Now the property of the Cape Cod National Seashore, the house is well maintained and open to the public during the summer season.

A close-up of the front door and two windows. The windows are nine panes over six panes, and the trim on all openings is sparse. The front is clapboarded and the rest of the house is shingled. The house and trim are painted a traditional mustard yellow.

This undated image shows the house, facing south, when it was an active residence (*courtesy of CCNS*).

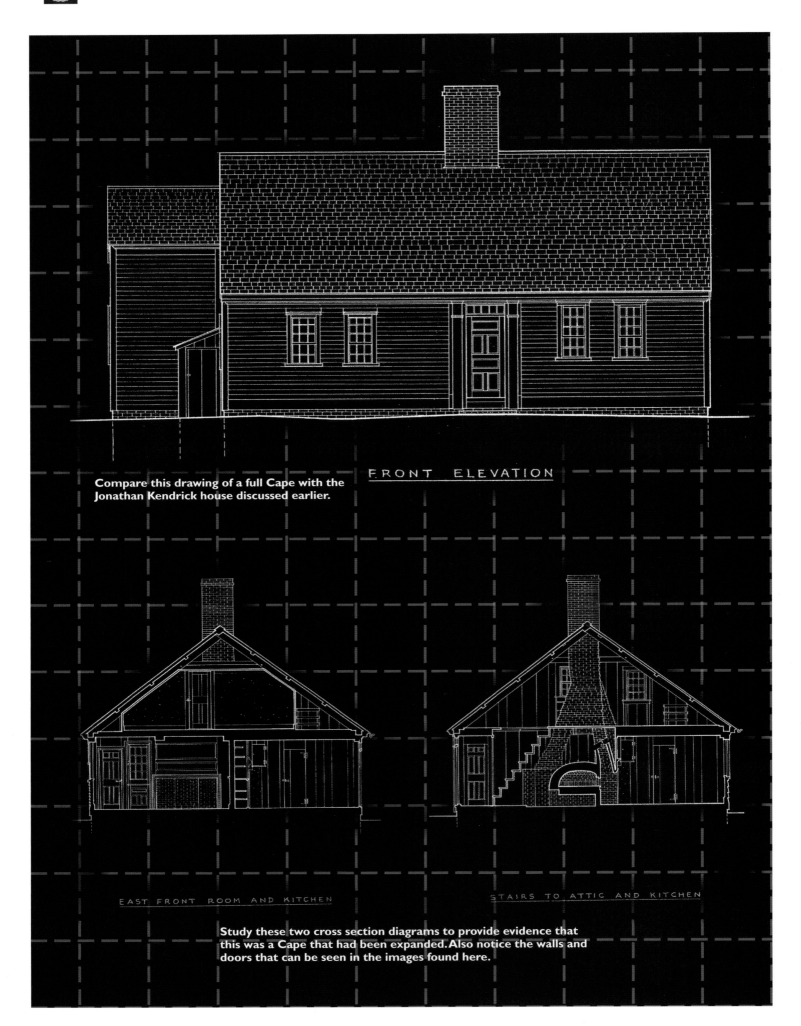

FRONT ELEVATION

Compare this drawing of a full Cape with the
Jonathan Kendrick house discussed earlier.

EAST FRONT ROOM AND KITCHEN

STAIRS TO ATTIC AND KITCHEN

Study these two cross section diagrams to provide evidence that
this was a Cape that had been expanded. Also notice the walls and
doors that can be seen in the images found here.

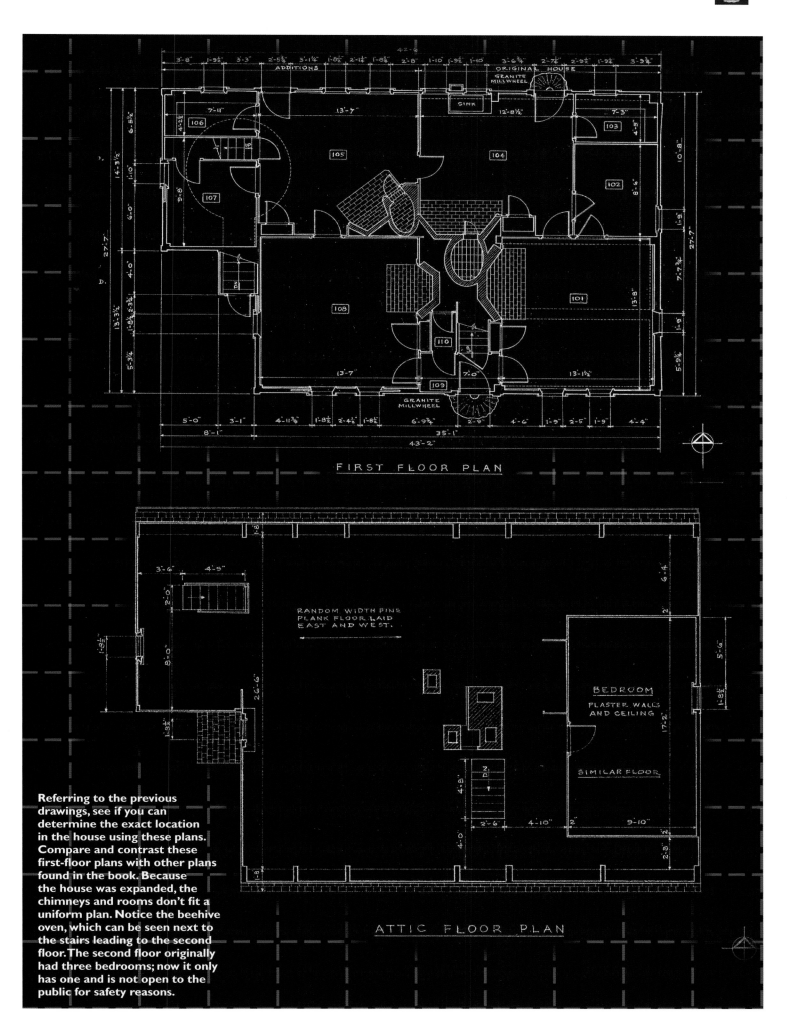

FIRST FLOOR PLAN

RANDOM WIDTH PINE
PLANK FLOOR LAID
EAST AND WEST.

BEDROOM

PLASTER WALLS
AND CEILING

SIMILAR FLOOR

ATTIC FLOOR PLAN

Referring to the previous drawings, see if you can determine the exact location in the house using these plans. Compare and contrast these first-floor plans with other plans found in the book. Because the house was expanded, the chimneys and rooms don't fit a uniform plan. Notice the beehive oven, which can be seen next to the stairs leading to the second floor. The second floor originally had three bedrooms; now it only has one and is not open to the public for safety reasons.

Two contemporary images of the rear keeping room in the newer part of the house. The white parlor is in front of this room through the door (*black and white courtesy of LOC, color image courtesy of CCNS*).

Two views, fifty years apart, of the keeping room at the rear of the original half Cape (*black and white courtesy of LOC*).

This room and fireplace is in front of the keeping room in the original portion of the house. Compare the cupboards in the different rooms (*courtesy of CCNS*).

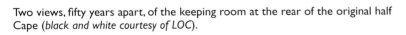

These two images, taken fifty years apart, show the new parlor at the front of the house. The front door can be seen through the hallway to the right. Stairs leading to the second floor are opposite the front door (*original courtesy of CCNS*).

Inside shutters, originally known as Indian shutters, were closed when attacked or in case of inclement weather. Found in early Capes, these shutters can also be seen in the John Newcomb House (page 112).

The chimney arrangement in the attic. In a house designed and built as a full Cape with a center chimney, there would have been one flue. The house never has had a central heating system (*courtesy of LOC*).

The second-floor bedroom. Notice the roof construction in this original part of the house and the lack of insulation. The window faces east (*courtesy of CCNS*).

Evidence of antiquity can be found throughout the house; the pantry door is just one example. Each panel in the door is a single piece of wood; the trim around each panel holds it in place. Notice the wide-plank floor boards. The rear door is to the left.

Looking down the narrow stairs; the door at the bottom opens opposite the front door (*courtesy of LOC*).

Compare these two images, taken a half-century apart, of the rear of the house.

An old privy, with a view, still sits on the grounds.

Jedediah Higgins House, 1730
Truro, Massachusetts

Several of the houses discussed and illustrated in this book were owned by members of the same family, such as the Doanes in Eastham or the Paines in Truro. This house was built by Jedediah Higgins and his brother, who had also built the Atwood-Higgins House in Wellfleet. While the Atwood-Higgins House seen on the previous pages was the result of an addition to an existing structure to make the house a full Cape, this house was originally constructed as a full Cape. Listed on the National Register of Historic Places, the house has been examined in detail and its history recorded. Much of the research was done when the Cape Cod National Seashore was in its formative stages. Major restoration work was done to preserve the property and, like several other homes in the Seashore, it is leased to a tenant. Situated halfway up a hill, the house faces south.

The east side of the house has two more smaller windows than the west side. A dormer has been added to the rear to increase head room in the bedrooms.

Sitting on a hill and facing south, the Jedediah Higgins house has an unusual arrangement in the spacing of the front windows (*black and white courtesy of LOC*).

These are the two small windows on the east side of the house. The pink room with the curtain is a bathroom.

A view out the front, side window on the west side of the house.

From the second floor, the narrow stairs lead down to the hallway and front door.

Two views captured by HABS shows the front room, which would have been a bedroom (*courtesy of LOC*).

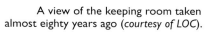

The other front room was the parlor (*courtesy of LOC*).

A view of the keeping room taken almost eighty years ago (*courtesy of LOC*).

Compare these diagrams of the house drawn in the 1930s to the actual present-day photographs *(courtesy of LOC).*

SOUTH ELEVATION

NORTH ELEVATION

WEST ELEVATION

Solomon Howes House, 1800
Chatham, Massachusetts

Now known as the Bow Roof House and presently a guest house for visitors to the Chatham area, this Cape was built in 1800 for the sea captain Solomon Howes. Howes, who along with his wife was about to leave on a long voyage, had given a "loyal friend" money with which to build him a mansion. Using the money more for drink, the friend only had enough funds to build this bow roof cottage. More ostentatious than a typical Cape, it certainly wasn't a house appropriate for a sea captain. Roam the nearby streets and several large colonials can be found that are similar to the type of property that Solomon Howes would have expected when he returned from sea. Facing south, with distant views of Oyster Pond, the house now sits shaded among the trees. Atypical of the style, the house has twin interior chimneys. The center entry front door is slightly offset to the west/left and has a four light transom with simple pilasters. A dentilated cornice is present beneath the roofline. It wasn't until after WWII that the house was modernized. Presently, the house is in excellent condition, well maintained, and available for occupancy as a bed and breakfast. It provides anyone the opportunity to live, albeit for a night or two, in a house more than two hundred years old.

A present-day view of the house hidden in the trees.

This photograph, more than seventy years old, is an image of the Solomon Howes house when it had clear views of nearby Oyster Pond. The small addition to the rear right has been renovated and enlarged with a subsequent addition to include several more bedrooms for guests *(courtesy of LOC).*

The most distinctive feature of this old Cape is the "rainbow roof." Built to emulate the bottom of a ship, this shape may have been thought to be more resistant to rain, wind, and snow. Aesthetically, it is obviously more attractive and harmonious than a typical slanted flat roof. Hundreds of years ago, when a bow roof was being planned for a house, the wood rafters would be cut and seasoned. This was the basic process: Placed across a block (about eighteen inches high) at about one third the length of the board, the rafters would be weighted at each end to create the bow after an extended period of time. The two color views are of the east and west side of the house (*plan courtesy of LOC*).

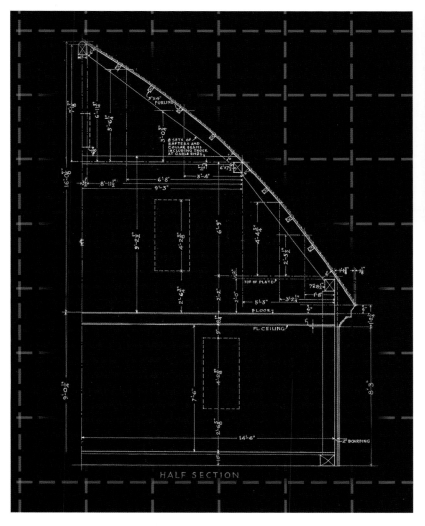

HALF SECTION

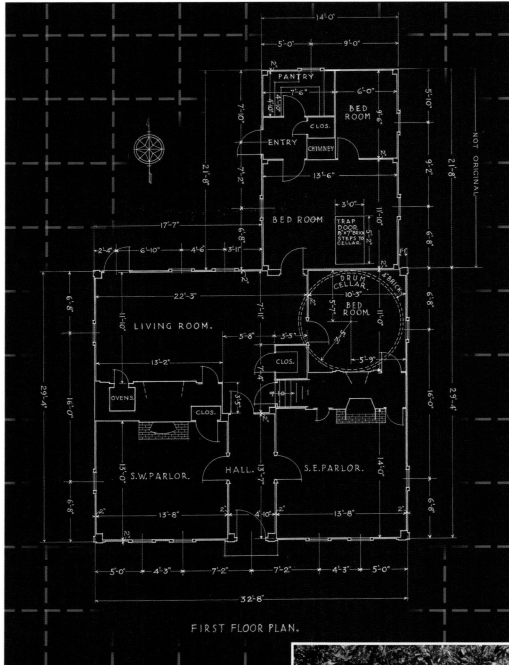

FIRST FLOOR PLAN.

A plan of the first floor; locate the following images from the different rooms. Notice the distinctive and unusual center hallway. Since the bedrooms have been renovated to include a bathroom, the room sizes are slightly different. Still, the fabric of the house remains in several rooms with beautifully maintained paneling, wide floor boards, and classic fireplaces. The recent addition to the rear, which has since been renovated, is now an open family room *(courtesy of LOC)*.

A view of the rear and west side of the house. Compare this arrangement of windows on the side to other Capes in this book. A shed dormer was recently added to the second floor.

Facing south, and exposed to the sun, the original front door requires continual attention.

A close-up detail of one of the doors leading into a bedroom.

These two views are of the southeast room, which is now a guest bedroom with twin beds. Opposite the beds is this large fireplace with a rare beehive oven. Expected in the keeping room where there is one, a second oven in this room is unusual. A bathroom to the far right replaced a closet. A Franklin fireplace had been installed to improve heating. The fireplaces are no longer used because of the danger of fire.

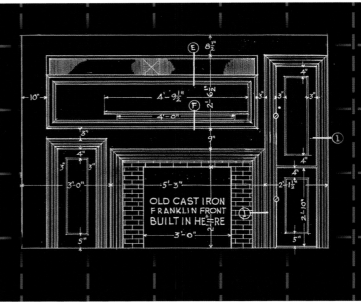

These two images show the other bedroom at the front of the house.
The door to the right of the fireplace leads to a recently added bathroom.
Occasionally, it is fairly easy, as in this case, to identify the Georgian
influence in the paneling. Compare the plan to the photograph to observe
how the wall has been altered (*plan courtesy of LOC*).

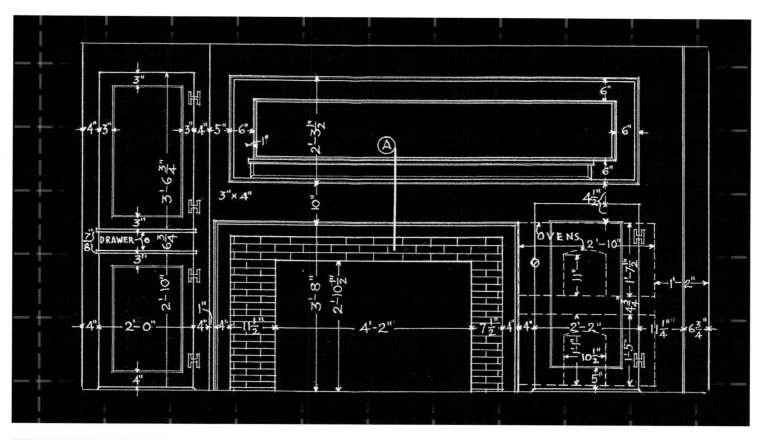

Three views of the keeping room with the second beehive oven. The window over the twin beds looks out on the rear of the house. The plan will give you some idea of the size of the wall, fireplace, and ovens (*plan courtesy of LOC*).

Jabez Wilder House, 1690
Hingham, Massachusetts

One of the most beautiful old Capes, this bowed-roof home, which is located on the main road leading into Hingham's town center, has been meticulously maintained. Built in 1690, the house was supposedly home, at one time, to as many as twenty-two Jabez Wilder family members.

Taken more than seventy years apart, these three images of the Jabez Wilder house still sustain the belief that this is one of the oldest and most stately of all Capes. Changes, additions, and modern improvements have only added to the sophistication of this home (*black and white courtesy of LOC*).

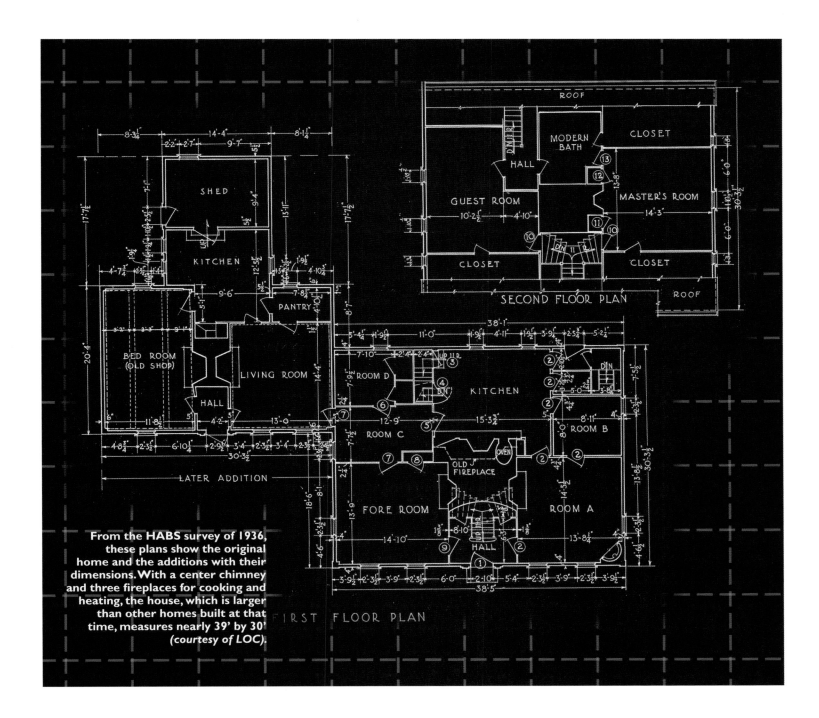

SECOND FLOOR PLAN

FIRST FLOOR PLAN

From the **HABS** survey of 1936, these plans show the original home and the additions with their dimensions. With a center chimney and three fireplaces for cooking and heating, the house, which is larger than other homes built at that time, measures nearly 39' by 30' *(courtesy of LOC)*.

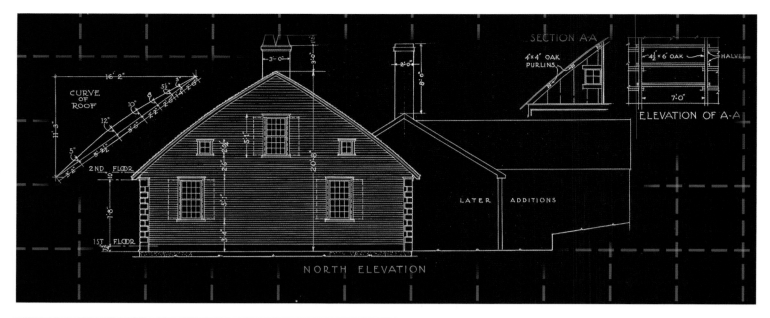

The distinctive bow roof can be seen in each side view of the house, as well as the dimensions in the plans from HABS. If a house was being planned, but was not to be built for more than a year, the roof rafters for the bow would be left outside, supported at a specific height (about 18", or a third of the way down the beam), and weighted at both ends. Over time, the rafter would slowly bend to the desired shape. Notice the quoins on the corners of the house, which were added later.

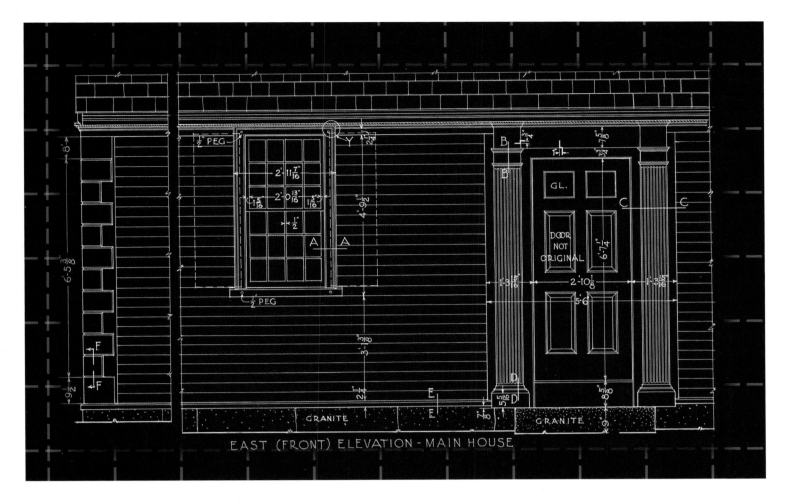

EAST (FRONT) ELEVATION - MAIN HOUSE

The addition and the ell to the back have traditional rooflines.

The granite step at the front door may be original, but the new door has pilasters that have been added to the trim.

Images shot for the HABS survey show the kitchen (notice the oven to the left), a corner cupboard, and the two rooms with fireplaces. Compare these images to the previous plans to identify their location in the house. Notice the wide-board floors and the painted rug (*courtesy of LOC*).

Parts of the modernized barn may be as old as the house.

The "good morning" front stairs were a later addition, opening to a bedroom on each side at the top (*plan courtesy of LOC*).

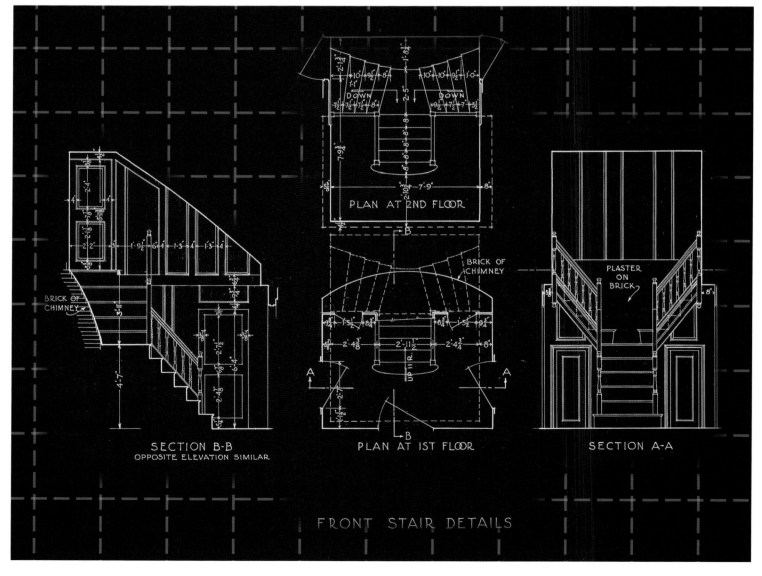

FRONT STAIR DETAILS

Additional Hingham Capes

Situated between Boston and Plymouth, Hingham, Massachusetts, with its large protected harbor, has attracted settlers ever since the first two colonies were established in the 1620s. Two of the oldest houses illustrated in this book are found in Hingham. Through the centuries, numerous Capes have been built in this community, and many are still standing, a testament to the quality of construction and the demand for the excellence of the Cape Cod style design. Through the years, they have been modernized for the ease of present-day living, but their historical fabric and classic simplicity remains. Compare these following eight homes built anywhere from the end of the eighteenth century until a third of the way through the nineteenth century. All are found on the main thoroughfares through the town.

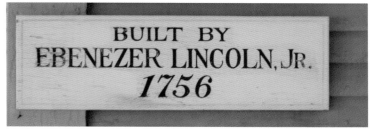

BUILT BY
EBENEZER LINCOLN, Jr.
1756

Ebenezer Lincoln was a relative of Samuel Lincoln, whose gambrel house is also illustrated in this book; this house is a full Cape with an addition to the rear. The front door with trim has a Georgian influence. Unlike most of the other Capes, it is not painted white.

This house, built in 1778, is the only three-quarter Cape in the group; there is a large addition to the rear.

Note the side door and the window at the peak of the house.

This Cape, built two hundred years ago (1811), has been impeccably restored.

Built in 1825, this house has similar sidelights to the previous Cape built in 1811.

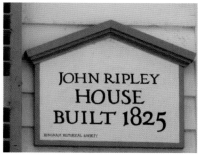

This full Cape has shutters on both the windows and the front door. The Hingham Historical Society assists homeowners in determining the year of construction of the house.

Another classic Cape without sidelights; this one was erected in 1833.

This Cape started out not as a house but as a store owned by Daniel Wilder, a descendent of Jabez Wilder, who had a nearby homestead

When Henry David Thoreau walked up from the beach more than one hundred and sixty years ago, this is the house that he saw, the former residence of the Wellfleet oysterman John Newcomb. Immortalized by Thoreau in his book *Cape Cod*, the house from the outside remains unchanged and is as Thoreau saw it. This image was taken before the famous hurricane of 1938, which blew over the tree at the end of the driveway (*courtesy of WHS*).

John Newcomb House, 1780
Wellfleet, Massachusetts

*Having walked about eight miles since we struck the beach...
we turned inland over barren hills and valleys...tracing up a
Hollow, discovered two or three sober-looking houses within
half a mile, uncommonly near the eastern coast. Their garrets
were apparently so full of chambers, that the roofs could hardly
lie down straight, and we did not doubt that there was room
for us there. Houses near the sea are generally low and broad.
These were a story and half high; but if you merely counted the
windows in their gable-ends, you would think that there were
many more stories...The great number of windows in the ends
of the houses, and their irregularity in size and position, here
and elsewhere on the Cape, struck us agreeably...There were
windows for grown folks and windows for the children...*

Henry David Thoreau made four journeys to Cape Cod, and
the 1849 description on page 38 describes the home pictured on
these pages, which was owned by a Wellfleet oysterman, John
Newcomb. Thoreau and his travelling companion on this trip,
William Ellery Channing, stayed here for a night. Thoreau later
wrote about his visits in the book *Cape Cod*. Reading *Cape Cod*
is worthwhile because it provides insight into a time and place
that no longer exists. Who nowadays would, without some
reluctance, welcome strangers who just walked up from the
beach into their home, provide them with food and a place to
sleep? And then upon their leaving, provide them with more
food?

Described as a Georgian Cape Cod double-house, the
best information suggests Newcomb's house was built between
1780 and 1790. The house, typical of early Capes, faces south.
With the exception of new windows and the two additions, the
house still retains its original character. The interior has been
modernized.

The Outer Cape, no longer barren and treeless, is covered with pitch pine and scrub oak forests. Trails and pathways wind through the woodlands that are now part of the Cape Cod National Seashore (CCNS). What was open and with wide vistas during Thoreau's time, now is wooded with a secluded landscape.

The present-day house, more than two hundred and twenty years old, is now surrounded by trees.

Taken more than fifty years apart, these two images are of the west side of the house (*black and white courtesy of LOC*).

Also taken fifty years apart, these images show the east side of the house, which is what Thoreau first saw when he walked up from the beach. Notice the very small window opening at the peak that Thoreau considered "strange" (*black and white courtesy of LOC*).

The front door reflects the Georgian influence that characterized houses built during that era.

The two front windows, with Indian shutters, are in the room where Thoreau and Channing slept. John Newcomb's wife may have closed the shutters during the night by sliding them across the inside of the windows. Shutters were also found on an upstairs bedroom. The original windows with nine panes over six have been replaced, but the shutters were kept.

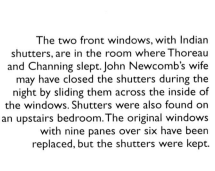

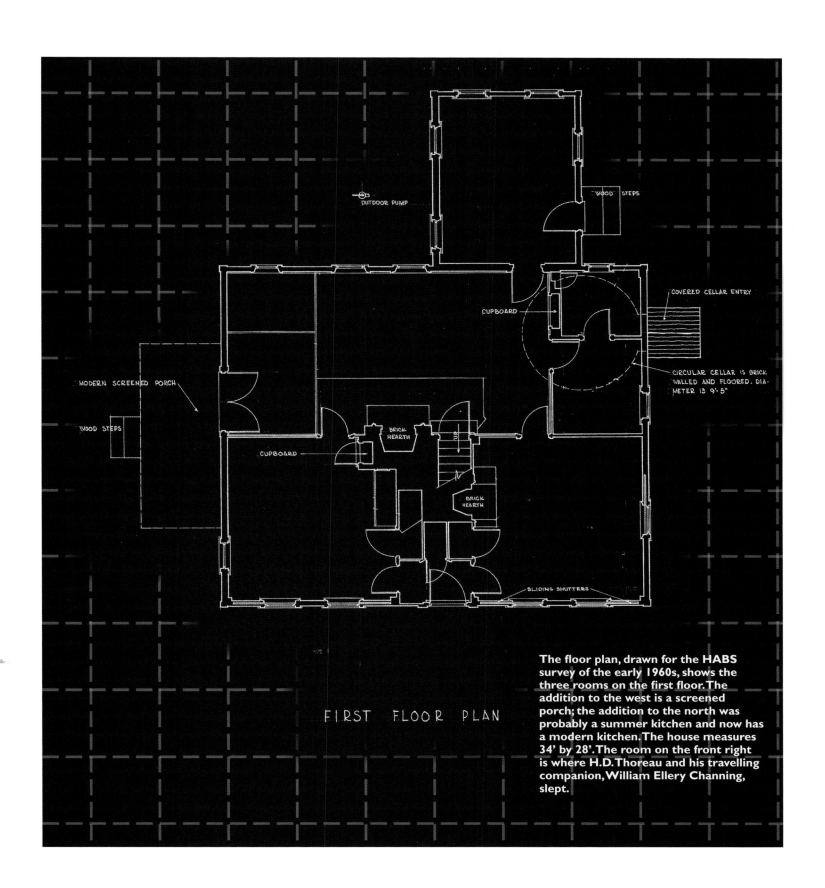

OUTDOOR PUMP

WOOD STEPS

COVERED CELLAR ENTRY

CUPBOARD

CIRCULAR CELLAR IS BRICK
WALLED AND FLOORED. DIA-
METER IS 9'-5"

MODERN SCREENED PORCH

WOOD STEPS

BRICK
HEARTH

CUPBOARD

BRICK
HEARTH

SLIDING SHUTTERS

FIRST FLOOR PLAN

The floor plan, drawn for the HABS
survey of the early 1960s, shows the
three rooms on the first floor. The
addition to the west is a screened
porch; the addition to the north was
probably a summer kitchen and now has
a modern kitchen. The house measures
34' by 28'. The room on the front right
is where H.D. Thoreau and his travelling
companion, William Ellery Channing,
slept.

The present-day narrow stairs lead from the kitchen in the rear of the house to the second floor. Originally, the stairs were probably behind the front door, as seen in the previous Atwood-Higgins house (page 85).

Wide-plank floors in the kitchen lead to the screened-in porch. Only a short distance from the Atlantic Ocean, these boards were once part of a sailing vessel, as evidenced by the damage done by shipworms.

More than one hundred fifty years ago, Thoreau may have looked out this west-facing window and wrote: "Our host took pleasure in telling us the names of the ponds, most of which we could see from his windows, and making us repeat them after him, to see if we got them right. They were Gull Pond, the largest and a very handsome one, clear and deep, and more than a mile in circumference, Newcomb's, Swett's, Slough, Horse-Leech, Round, and Herring Ponds, all connected at high water." Now only one pond is visible when the leaves are on the trees. This view is looking out the windows toward the west.

Taken in the early 1960s, this image shows the rear of the house with the two additions. Notice the well pump in the foreground and the clapboards, which are usually found on the front of the house. The other sides of the house are covered with shingles (*courtesy of LOC*).

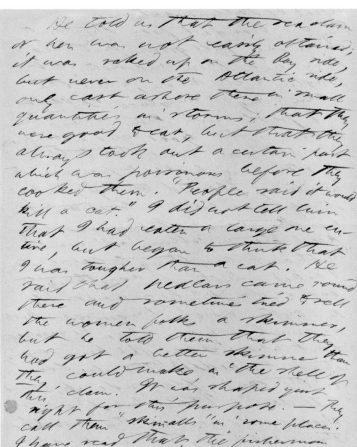

"He told us that the sea clam…" so wrote Thoreau on his visit to Wellfleet. This actual page from Thoreau's writings is on display at the Wellfleet Historical Society. If you look carefully, you can see that he wrote on both sides of the paper.

An image of the interior of a relatively recent addition to the east end of the main house, which has utilized old beams and boards.

Solomon Doane House, 1750
Eastham, Massachusetts

We usually don't think of houses as being related, but in the case of this, and several other homes in Eastham, there is a distinct connection. Deacon John Doane, one of the founding families in 1644, and his relatives built a variety of Capes in town, several of which are identified in this book. This full Cape was built by Solomon Doane in 1750 and remained in the family until 1947, when it was sold to the present owners. This house was built on part of a two-hundred acre farm that was originally owned by his great-grandfather Deacon John Doane. Although unproven, it is believed that a part of this Cape was supposedly moved here from the original Doane Homestead (1640s). At the time this house was built, the neighborhood included a windmill, a school, and a number of other farm homes. Described in the literature as a bow-roof Cape, the curve in this roof is not as obvious as that in the Jabez Wilder house (page 102). The exterior detail is limited and fenestration (the placement of windows in a building) is varied. The historic vestiges of the house that remain in the interior are its hand-hewn wall boards, wide-plank floors and "good morning" stairs. In 1951, the house was moved back from the road, placed on a poured concrete foundation (facing east), the chimney and flues were repaired and rebuilt, and the property was significantly renovated with new additions. Well maintained, this is an excellent example of a typical full Cape from the Outer Cape region. In addition, there is some evidence that H. D. Thoreau may have stayed here on his visits to the Cape in the 1850s.

Originally facing south to take advantage of the prevailing cooling winds in the summer and the warming sun in the winter, this house was moved back from the street in the early 1950s. Note and count the second floor windows and compare those present to the more recent image (*courtesy of EHS*).

The present-day house, now hidden from the street.

The front door with sidelights and a clamshell design above it.

The hardware on the front door is thought to be original.

When the house was being re-shingled, a small hidden window in an upstairs bedroom was discovered and is now open to the outside.

The narrow front stairs, directly behind the front door, lead to two bedrooms on the second floor.

The fireplace in the living room is not original because it had to be replaced when the house was moved. It is, though, an almost exact replica. Closer inspection finds an oven inside the fireplace that was used successfully during a recent power outage.

Good morning! The two front bedrooms on the second floor have a door that opens to the front stairs, which occasioned the early-in-the-day greeting.

A small attic window in one of the rear additions is tucked under the eave.

To the left of the front door is the parlor. This fireplace, as well as four others in the house, leads to the central chimney flue. All are in excellent condition and draw without any problems. Note the clamshell design in the cupboard.

This is not an image of a view in the attic or in the barn but in the cellar underneath the parlor. When the house was moved, it was placed on a poured concrete foundation; these are the joists found under the floor. Other old Capes in the area that don't have foundations can also be found to have tree trunks for support.

The present-day owners discovered this grinding wheel while gardening. Discarded years ago and long forgotten, it was found near the barn, which has not been moved.

The nearby barn may be older than the house. Notice how the beams are connected and a peg can be seen on the bottom.

Nickerson/Gregory House, 1746
Provincetown, Massachusetts

Provincetown, at the outermost tip of the Cape, was one of the first areas to be explored by Europeans, but one of the last to be settled, developed, and incorporated. Although it was visited and named by Bartholomew Gosnold in the early 1600s, it was the Pilgrims in 1620 that briefly stayed and explored the region before sailing across the bay and settling in Plymouth. Later on, this area became known as the Provincelands (which originally included Truro), and dwellings were built along the shore with only boats for transportation. There were no roads and the houses faced the water. By 1680, the community was made up of fisherman, smugglers, outlaws, and "mooncussers," who supposedly used lanterns to lure ships to wreck on the beach at night and then salvaged the cargo and parts of the ship, which were cut up and used in a variety of buildings. Old houses still standing today have the ribs and remnants of these ships that were stranded on the beach. The earliest houses built, simple shacks, were located on the harbor and with constant tides and shifting sands were always threatened, so no evidence remains of them today. As the town became increasingly settled, more permanent residences would be constructed. The oldest house in town still standing is the Nickerson/Gregory house, built in 1746. Peaked Hill Bars, in the Atlantic Ocean east of the town, was the graveyard of many a ship. Some of the timbers and ribs of those wrecks can be found in this house, particularly the door frames. In addition, because the house was built on sand, crisscrossed log timbers were used to support the center chimney; the house, thirty feet wide and twenty-eight feet deep, was constructed around it. The original builder and owner, Seth Nickerson, was a ship's carpenter and used those skills to construct this dwelling. He collected heavy oak timbers for parts of the frame and wide pine boards for the flooring. From the early 1930s until 1992, when he passed away, John "Jack" Gregory, a prolific and well-known photographer, occupied the house, which was open to the public. It is now privately owned and still retains its original character more than two hundred and fifty years later.

This present day panorama of Provincetown Harbor, with the houses along the shore, is distinctively different from when this area of the Cape was first settled. Now tightly packed, houses and buildings line the deep safe harbor that has attracted fisherman for hundreds of years. The Pilgrim Monument stands in the distance near the center of town.

Two images taken nearly seventy years apart show the Nickerson/Gregory house. The old image is a postcard of the house when John Gregory, a renowned local photographer, had the residence open as a studio, a gallery, and also for tours. From the early 1930s, Gregory simply had to walk across the street to capture the beauty of Provincetown. For more than sixty years the house, now privately owned, was open to the public.

Narrow streets and houses tightly packed together are common throughout Provincetown. The east side of this house, which features fenestration similar to other large Capes, is nearly on the street; four granite blocks provide protection from vehicles.

A view of the west side of the house with beach roses in bloom

The front of the house. Notice how the roofline extends down to the top of the windows. The front door with four window lights and wood trim shows minimal ornamentation.

Additional Provincetown Capes

In addition to the Gregory/Nickerson House, along Commercial Street, and primarily in the West End, there are numerous old Capes built on the side of the street away from the water. The original fishing shacks, built before there were streets, were not substantial, fell into disrepair, and eventually disappeared. More suitable homes were built that would endure the conditions created by wind and water. Compare these six Capes, some used as guest houses today, which can easily be found walking the streets of the town at the tip of the Cape. Two significant characteristics that appear in some of these houses are the presence of dormers, so the resident/occupant on the second floor can look out on the water, and the fan-shaped light above the front door. The white picket fences, originally built to hold back the shifting sands, mark the edge of the sidewalk.

A blue plaque on the front of old Provincetown homes identifies the age of the house and features a sailing ship. Note the dentil molding. The dormers provide a view of the harbor across the street.

This Cape, built in 1807, is a guest house that has three upstairs rooms with water views.

This full Cape, built in the late 1790s, has some intriguing features: the top of the chimney, usually painted in black, is painted to match the trim; the small window on the second story looks like it must be on floor level; and the space between the front door and the two closest windows is not equal. That said, this is still a quaint, picturesque Cape.

Tucked between larger houses and behind a white picket fence, this Cape, built in 1820, has a similar door to the 1790 house.

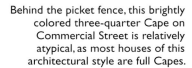

Behind the picket fence, this brightly colored three-quarter Cape on Commercial Street is relatively atypical, as most houses of this architectural style are full Capes.

Notice the distance between the top of the window and the roofline; this results in more headroom on the second floor. Just across the street is Provincetown Harbor. An addition to the rear adds more living space.

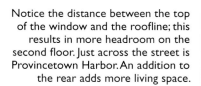

Elkanah Higgins House, 1783
Eastham, Massachusetts

This 1880s image of the Higgins house shows a typical three-quarter Cape. The barn in the background no longer exists. Closer examination of the left side of the house shows the roofline for the addition (*image courtesy of EHS*).

Through the years, many of the old Capes found in this book have been bought and sold, with different families owning the original house, which may have been built centuries ago. This house is different. This original three-quarter Cape has been in the same family since it was built by Elkanah Higgins in 1783. Over time, the house has been changed and updated as can be seen in these images. Although it was a year-round residence until relatively recently, the Cape is now only used during the summer season.

This present-day view shows two significant alterations to the house. First, a small window has replaced the front door; second, a door and two first-floor windows have been added to the side. This door opens to the original keeping room.

Another front view shows the shed addition. Notice the lilac bush and the daylilies that were favorite plantings of the early settlers.

The rear of the house with the driveway in the foreground.

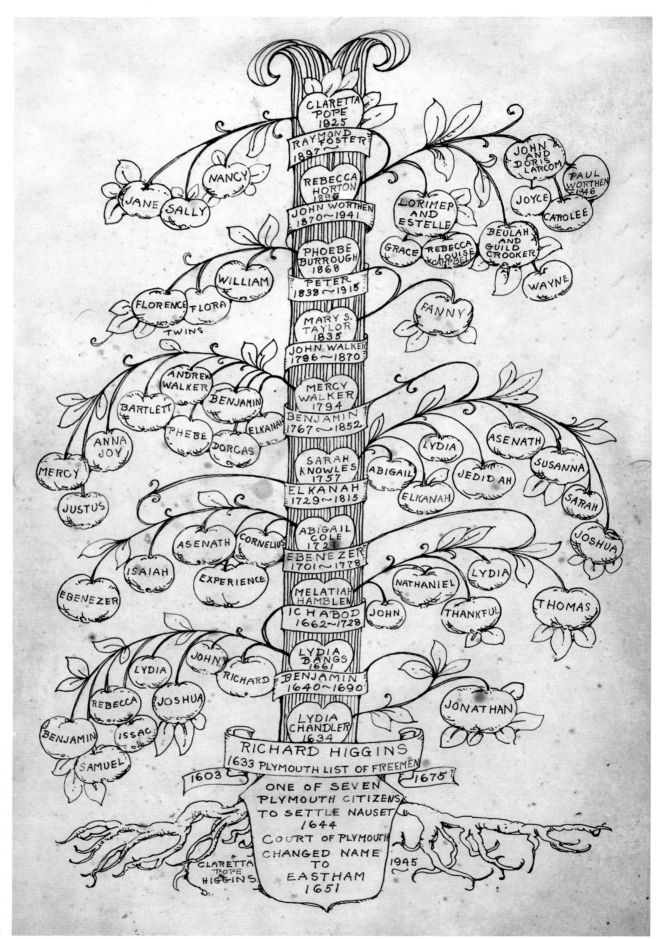

Unlike many of the other Capes featured here, this house has been in the same family since it was built. A family tree begins with the first settlers in Eastham in 1644 and continues to the present-day at the top.

An old stenciled chest found in the living room.

Narrow stairs with no railing lead to the second floor. Turn around from this view and you would be able to look out the small front window, where the front door originally was. Painting projects sometimes resulted in a unique arrangement of colors to finish several cans of paint.

For occupants that were not able to buy them, "rugs" would be painted on the floor. Later, knit rugs would cover the floor.

Found throughout the house, these stencils on walls and doors were painted by a family from a previous generation. Note the basic closet door.

At the top of the stairs are two bedrooms. The windows have a west-facing view. The large post in the middle is the chimney flue.

Doane House, 1680
Eastham, Massachusetts

This three-quarter Cape, maybe the oldest extant house in Eastham, is also a Doane house—it was built by a son of Deacon Doane. Whatever the true history of the building is, the fact that remains is that this house is not only one of the most picturesque but one of the best preserved in town. Modified and modernized over the last half-century, this Cape still retains characteristics of when it was built more than three hundred years ago. Note the unusual location of the offset chimney. Trim is sparse and with limited detail. Interior details include wide-board flooring, doors with original hardware, and paneling in the living room that suggest the early date of construction. The house has been in the present owner's family since 1929 and is now used as a summer residence.

The house faces south and is now surrounded by trees within the Cape Cod National Seashore. The brick patio is a relatively recent addition.

The east side of the home with a new bow window. Successive additions have been added to the side and rear.

The west side of the house and the ells that were added to the rear.

This outbuilding has been remodeled to be a guest house; it was built with lumber from an original barn that was taken down years ago.

Inside, the angled stairs lead to the second floor; the roof and beam can be seen in the upper middle section of the image. The window in this photograph is the one to the right of the front door in the outside view of the Cape.

Richard Paine House, 1719
Truro, Massachusetts

The Richard Paine house is seen in these two images taken nearly a half a century apart (*black and white courtesy of LOC*).

This may be the oldest existing Cape house in Truro. Similar to the Doane houses of Eastham, this is one of several Paine houses in Truro. The following text documents the arrangement between Thomas Paine II, housewright, and the future owner of a property that was to be built in Truro.

> *…build and set up and finish all below the chamber floor, one house or messauge of the dimensions and particular description following. Twenty three feet square on the ground floor, ten feet post, hemlock timber and boarding boards, the roof and front side to be shingled with pine shingles, the two ends and the back to be covered with cedar shingles, finish the lower part of the house into one front room, one kitchen, two bedrooms, one butry, front and end entry, two flights of stairs if needed and plain the boards for a chamber floor, the front room and the kitchen to be ceiled up to the windows, glass closet door in the front room, iron latches for all the doors, seven by nine glass for all the windows, a common cellar under the house, with a cellar house outside.*

This original house, built in the 1840s for $450.00, is no longer standing. But there are still several identifiable Paine houses in the area.

About twenty-four feet by twenty-nine feet in size, there are no known early images of this property. The house has been recently and extensively renovated; town records date the initial construction as 1719. Located on the stage coach line, this three-quarter Cape was also the local post office (the room to the right of the house, the west side) and a general store. The house was in the Paine family until the late 1800s. A permanent year-round residence for many years, the house is now available as a summer rental.

This image (1960) of the east side of the house shows a distinctive window that was added between the original second floor windows.

In this HABS image of the keeping room, notice the random-width flooring and the wood paneling to the left of the fireplace (*courtesy of LOC*).

Many of the older homes on the Outer Cape contain boards and beams from shipwrecked vessels. Stranded and broken-up ships were quickly salvaged not only for their cargo, but also for their wood. Several varieties of hardwood were used in the construction of sailing ships and made excellent building materials. This tapered corner post originally came from a ship.

Two views, taken years apart, show the front room that was then a parlor and is now a bedroom. Notice the Christian door that opens to a hallway and the front door (*courtesy of LOC*).

Samuel Paine House, 1825
Truro, Massachusetts

Fifty years ago, the HABS survey for the Library of Congress, in anticipation of the inception of the National Seashore, identified, examined, and collected information relative to those properties that were considered historically significant. The Samuel Paine House in Truro was one of those selected. Built in 1825, more than a century after the nearby Richard Paine House was constructed, this house still displays characteristics of the historical influence from the era when it was built.

This classic full Cape, with Greek Revival influence, seems only to improve with age. The black and white was taken as part of the HABS survey in 1960 (*courtesy of LOC*).

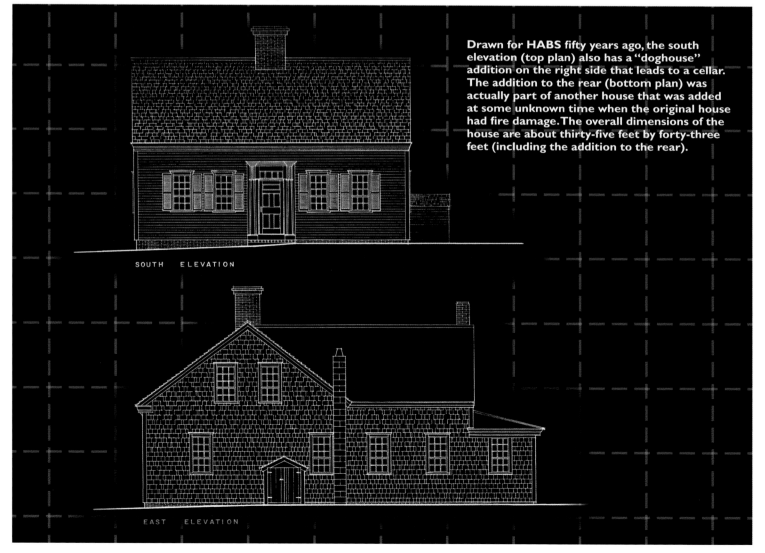

Drawn for HABS fifty years ago, the south elevation (top plan) also has a "doghouse" addition on the right side that leads to a cellar. The addition to the rear (bottom plan) was actually part of another house that was added at some unknown time when the original house had fire damage. The overall dimensions of the house are about thirty-five feet by forty-three feet (including the addition to the rear).

SOUTH ELEVATION

EAST ELEVATION

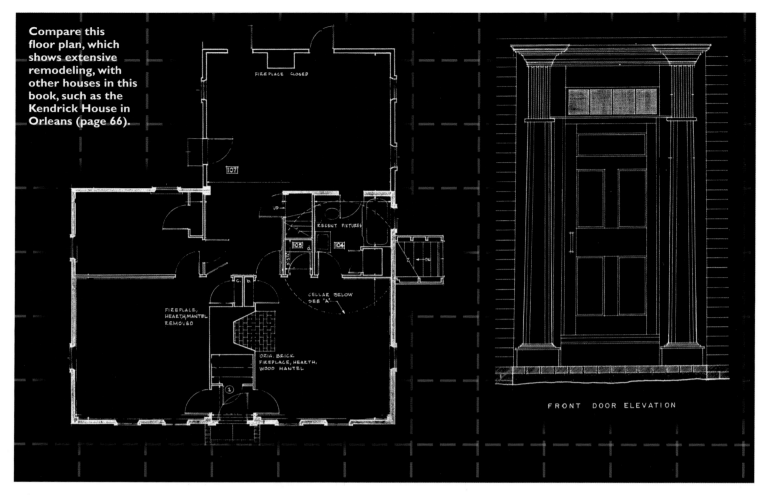

Compare this floor plan, which shows extensive remodeling, with other houses in this book, such as the Kendrick House in Orleans (page 66).

FRONT DOOR ELEVATION

Three different views of the front door with a four-light transom. Tapered wood molding is found on the flanking pilasters, which support an entablature over the entrance (*black and white and plan courtesy of LOC*).

Excluding the trees that have grown through the years, the east side of the well-maintained house looks unchanged over the last half-century (*black and white courtesy of LOC*).

A view of the east room with the fireplace and the cupboard; the door to the right led to the original keeping room. The front wall to the left had wood wainscoting to the height of the window stool. Note the painted wide-plank floor. Identify the location of this room on the previous floor plan (*courtesy of LOC*).

The north side view of the house and a new addition (*black and white courtesy of LOC*).

Venus Thompson House, 1700
Middleboro, Massachusetts

There are numerous old Cape-style houses in eastern Massachusetts and on Cape Cod with a documented pedigree that may date back more than three centuries. Any one of those could be included in this book. One parameter that was used to select which houses to include in this book was whether the property had ever been identified, examined, and photographed by the Historic American Building Survey (HABS). The qualified professionals, including historians, architects, and photographers, who surveyed the property provided accurate information about the house. This house, in a rural area of Middleboro, was investigated in the mid 1930s. Supposedly built around 1700, the property was identified as the Venus Thompson House. Venus was born in 1842, the great-great granddaughter of the original owner/builder of the house. Many facets of the house indicate an early construction date; some can be seen in these images.

The front door with five-panel sidelights on each side.

A present-day view of the Venus Thompson House.

Unchanged through the years, the Venus Thompson house is still in farm country, and horses are trained and stabled on the property.

The house faces east and towards the road in this 1934 HABS photograph (*courtesy of LOC*).

A rear view of the house with the addition, which features a modern kitchen.

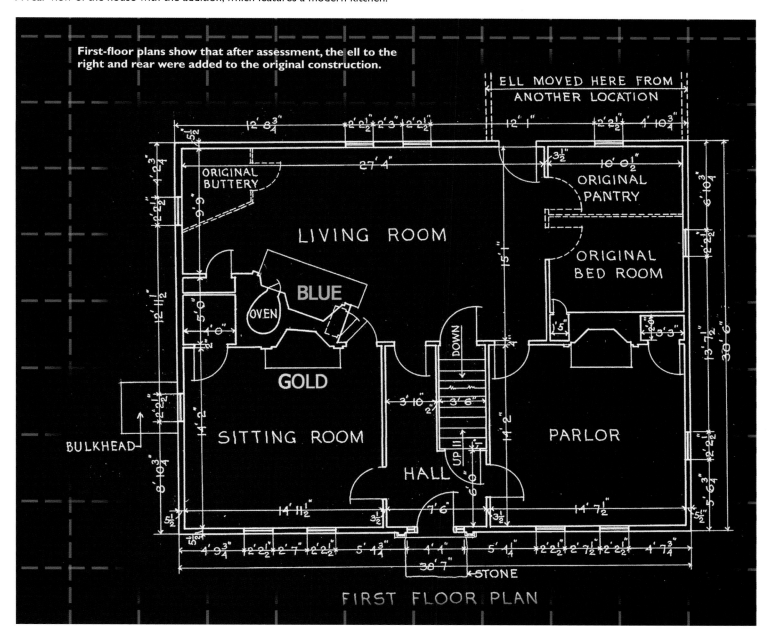

First-floor plans show that after assessment, the ell to the right and rear were added to the original construction.

ELL MOVED HERE FROM ANOTHER LOCATION

ORIGINAL BUTTERY

LIVING ROOM

ORIGINAL PANTRY

ORIGINAL BED ROOM

BLUE

OVEN

GOLD

BULKHEAD

SITTING ROOM

DOWN

UP

HALL

PARLOR

STONE

FIRST FLOOR PLAN

Two fireplaces found in the original house, and still functional, are found in what was the original keeping room (blue in previous plan) and what is now a bedroom (gold) showing how room use may change. Notice the wood paneling next to both fireplaces.

A quaint functional fireplace can be found on the second floor. The window in the background has a view to the north; compare this to the 1934 view.

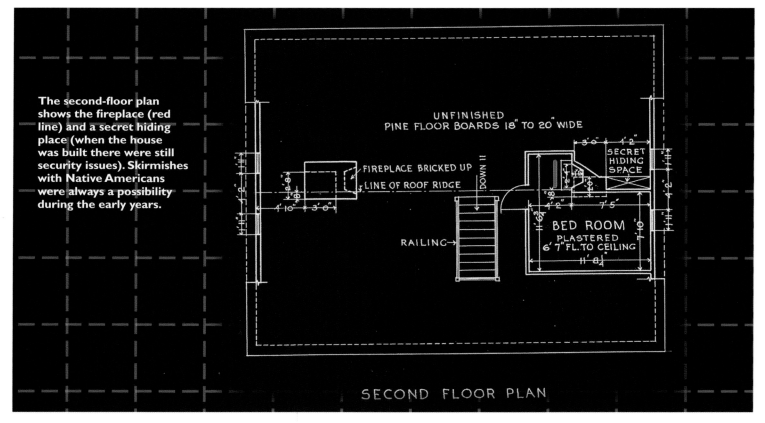

The second-floor plan shows the fireplace (red line) and a secret hiding place (when the house was built there were still security issues). Skirmishes with Native Americans were always a possibility during the early years.

UNFINISHED
PINE FLOOR BOARDS 18" TO 20" WIDE

FIREPLACE BRICKED UP
LINE OF ROOF RIDGE

DOWN 11

SECRET HIDING SPACE

RAILING→

BED ROOM
PLASTERED
6' 7" FL. TO CEILING

SECOND FLOOR PLAN

Winthrop House
Eighteenth Century
Plympton, Massachusetts

West of Plymouth, many of the towns are still rural, with farms and cranberry bogs. Older homes in these communities have been lived in and maintained for centuries. This full Cape, as well as several others in town, was built by the descendants of John Winthrop, who arrived from England in 1630 and became one of the most important Massachusetts political figures of his time. More than two hundred years later, this Cape, with its simplicity of architectural design, fits into its treed setting. Compare the angle of the roof and the size of this house with other full Capes in this book. A view of the west side shows a new larger window has been added to the keeping room. An addition to the rear, with a large modern kitchen, provides more living space. The original fireplace, still used during the winter months, has a baking oven. A functional privy, no longer necessary, can be found by walking in the woods behind the house.

Just down the street is this similar vintage old house.

Freeman House, 1726
East Sandwich, Massachusetts

As different areas of the Cape were settled, increased in population, and eventually became incorporated, these towns developed, led by different families making significant contributions to their communities. Some of these individuals may have been builders. Many of the houses that were built more than two hundred and fifty years are still standing. In Eastham, Higgins and Doane are identified with numerous houses, in Truro, Paine houses are common, and in this three-quarter Cape in Sandwich, the house is associated with the Freeman family. At the rear of the house, and not readily visible or distinguishable from the exterior, is a room that possibly dates back to the late 1600s. It may have been built and occupied before the large Cape you see here was built.

Narrow stairs lead to the second floor.

This view of the west side of the house shows an addition to the rear that has a modern kitchen. The addition to the right leads to a barn that was constructed to house a thriving business. Compare the windows on the second floor on this side to the other side of this house and to other Capes in the text, such as the Jedediah Higgins or Thomas Newcomb houses.

The front of the house. The narrow windows, about eight inches below the cornice, are typical of Capes of this era.

The left side of the house faces east, the front faces north. Houses on the Cape, being exposed to severe weather conditions, constantly require shingles and clapboards to be replaced. Here, the roof has been recently shingled

These adze marks, found on the end of one of the beams, are located to the right of the fireplace. Was the house flaked (moved)? Each beam in the room is marked to indicate its position relative to the other beams. Note the primitive door in the corner.

A view of the fireplace in the oldest room in the house. Note the beamed ceiling.

Additional Sandwich Capes

A short ride from the Plimoth Colony, Sandwich was one of the first areas settled in what is now Cape Cod. Interest in the area developed when it was found that there was access to Buzzard's Bay and ships no longer had to navigate around the dangerous shoals off the Cape. Both Bourne and Sandwich have some of the oldest properties on the Cape.

Eighteenth Century
King's Highway, Yarmouth, Massachusetts

As more Europeans arrived in the New World, more colonies, such as the Massachusetts Bay Colony, were formed and the settlers expanded into other regions. Colonists formed communities all along the eastern seaboard, as far south as what is now Florida. From the Plymouth Bay Colony, expansion moved west and also south towards the Cape. Sandwich, being closest to Plymouth, was one of the first towns settled on the Cape. Of all the roads built to connect the communities, one old road remains today, King's Highway, also identified as Route 6A (on Cape Cod) on maps. Beginning in Sandwich, near the Cape Cod Canal, the road winds along the north shore of the Cape through towns and settlements that were once the center of business and activities. (The Cape Cod Canal, about a century old, was first proposed by Myles Standish as early as the late 1620s to facilitate commerce between Plymouth and New York). King's Highway terminates as a road in Orleans; its exact path north to Provincetown is lost in history. Sections of a road identified as 6A in Truro and Provincetown are probably not the thoroughfare the colonists used. Today, traveling along King's Highway, the observer passes through history and drives by homes, inns, and other buildings, some more than two hundred and fifty years old. Two short sections of the olde highway in Yarmouth are illustrated here.

A granite marker along King's Highway indicates the distance to Plymouth and Provincetown.

Compare these two images of a section of King's Highway in Yarmouth, shot more than one hundred years apart. Three lovely Capes, well maintained, are found along this stretch of the highway. On the south side of the road, this view of the old homes is looking west. Nearby, years ago, was a busy harbor with sailing packets that would travel back and forth to Boston. Many sections, along the highway and in the different towns are part of a historical district with covenants and jurisdiction regarding property maintenance. Notice the houses' proximity to the street.

THIS PROPERTY HAS BEEN
PLACED ON THE
NATIONAL REGISTER
OF HISTORIC PLACES
BY THE UNITED STATES
DEPARTMENT OF THE INTERIOR

This house, a large three-quarter Cape, also has a large central chimney with flues from three rooms. An addition to the rear is not visible in this image. Notice the metal plaque to the left of the front door, which indicates that this house is listed on the National Register of Historic Places (NRHP). Extensive documentation and time is spent to determine the authenticity and significance of a property and if it should be included on the National Register.

The next house is also a three-quarter Cape with an ell to the rear. The interesting historical commentary on the house is the white chimney with the black top, signifying that the original owners (as of 1775) were Tory sympathizers. In contrast, the previous house (as of today) with the plain chimney was sympathetic to the revolution. Small vents, instead of windows, are found on the second floor.

The third house in this group is a half Cape (three bay: two windows and a door) and the most common configuration of this style, with the door on the right. The chimney on this home, listed on the NRHP, also indicates the year it was built. Notice the side is clapboarded instead of shingled. The addition (three-quarter Cape) to the right was added later.

A second section of the King's Highway in Yarmouth, looking east, with three old homes, all of which are listed on the NRHP. Compare these three Capes, built about the same time in the 1740s, and check the differences. Further east on the Outer Cape, rocks were scarce and at a premium for building; in this region, they were more abundant and could be used in the rock wall in front of the first half Cape.

Three nice half Capes, with Georgian-influenced trim, are distinctively different. Observe the middle house, which unlike its neighbors has the door on the right. Did the original builder/owner decide, "I'm going to be a little bit different than my neighbor?" All are well maintained, with ells to the rear, and show minimal modern improvements.

Two additional views of the third Cape, perhaps built more than a quarter of a millennium ago, but still attractive and stylish.

Hidden among the trees, this three-quarter Cape looks similar to other houses in the neighborhood. On the side view, note the shingled roof on the addition and the total of three chimneys. On the left of the image are minimal views of two of its closest neighbors.

Larger than the previous Capes, note the distance between the windows and roofline; this home has two additional small windows on the right side of the second floor. Successive additions have expanded this house, which is also listed on the NRHP.

Compare and contrast these two full Capes. Which one is older? Why the difference in the number and location of chimneys from a standard full Cape? Were these houses originally half the size and expanded?

Higgins House, 1800 Wellfleet, Massachusetts

When one sees an old full Cape, one of the first questions regarding its construction that seems to arise is, "Was this built as a smaller house and expanded, or is it original throughout?" Was this house similar to the Atwood-Higgins, described previously, or built as you see it? And the answer is, this full Cape was built as a full Cape. A recent historical examination of the north side sheathing and in the roof boards, rafters, and

The front door, with Federal influence, is wider than the traditional front door on a Cape. Usually, the front doors are thirty-two inches and not bigger than thirty-four inches, and this one is wider than that.

purlins, indicate that they were uniform throughout and showed no evidence of a change in character that would have indicated an addition. The lumber used was new at construction. The house in the Federal style, in fact, may have been built as early as 1780. Examination of the floor joists revealed that all were new when built and show no evidence of used timbers; they were thirty inches on center, which was common for two centuries and may have been derived from an old English measure. One of the finest homes on the Lower Cape, this house, with exterior and interior architectural details, is grander and more magnificent than its contemporaries.

Most of the homes seen in this book were probably part of a farm and not built particularly close to water. Houses near the Atlantic Ocean were constructed away from the water and in the lee of a hill to avoid the winds of the winter storms. On the Cape Cod Bay side, houses would be built near harbors as residences for people involved in fishing and salt works. The original occupants may very well have worked in either of these industries, as the house is less than a stone's throw from the water (Wellfleet Harbor and nearby Cape Cod Bay).

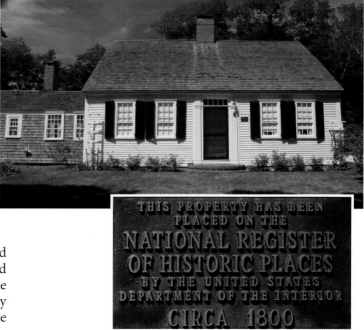

The front of the house faces the local creek, and more than two-hundred years ago, instead of a salt marsh, a boat may have been docked here. Listed on the NRHP, the house may even date prior to the designation on the plaque.

The north side of the house, with a window arrangement commonly found in full Capes. The front of the house is to the left. Note the small "doghouse" on the rear wall, which leads to a food storage cellar nine feet in diameter.

A window on the rear of the house with nine panes over six; each pane, at seven by nine inches, is larger than usual glass.

The rear of the house with the addition, to the right, that was added about eighty years ago.

The addition to the rear was built in the 1930s; a copy of the *New York Times* was found during the historical examination. A previous owner first used the addition as an art studio. Famous for its quality of light, the Outer Cape has drawn the visual artist to this area for more than a century. With an art school begun in nearby Provincetown in the late 1800s, the Cape has attracted painters to capture these local vistas. Now the addition houses a kitchen.

Sylvanus Doane House, 1767
Eastham, Massachusetts

When the Cape Cod National Seashore was being proposed, this house was one of the properties that was part of the HABS survey team that included historians and architects. Conjecture as to the date of construction and the original style of the house were included in the study of this house. Although we may never know the exact date the house was built, evidence is present that indicates that Obadiah Doane, son of Sylvanus Doane, was born here in 1767. The architectural historians' examination revealed that the method of construction and details present indicate the house was built later in the eighteenth century. They also determined that the original structure was a "house" or half Cape and added onto in subsequent years. Originally, the house was twenty-eight feet by twenty-two feet but is now thirty-seven feet by twenty-two feet. The additions, in feet, are approximately twelve by fourteen and sixteen by twenty-four. The following images and plans show evidence that the house had been enlarged to its present dimensions. The west ell was added sometime around 1900; it is unknown when the house was expanded to a full Cape as seen now. This is one of the several Doane houses found in Eastham described in this book.

Compare these three images of the Sylvanus Doane house for the changes that have occurred in the past eighty years. The rear chimney on the main house has been removed, a door and window have been reversed on the ell addition, there are now vent pipes on the roof for the plumbing, and the nearby trees have grown significantly. Note, also, the windows on the second floor are six over nine panes, instead of the normal configuration of nine over six (*black and white courtesy of EHS*).

Compare these two views of the front of the house taken fifty years apart. This black and white image, as well as other similar photographs of the house, was captured when the Cape Cod National Seashore was in its formative stage and a survey was done of significant historical properties (*black and white courtesy of LOC*).

SOUTH ELEVATION

Preserved for future generations, this plan and the two images of the sides of the house depict how the house was in 1960. It is possible to record the changes that have occurred in the last fifty years. On the plan, note the bulkhead on the east side of the house, which was the oldest and original part of the property (*courtesy of LOC*).

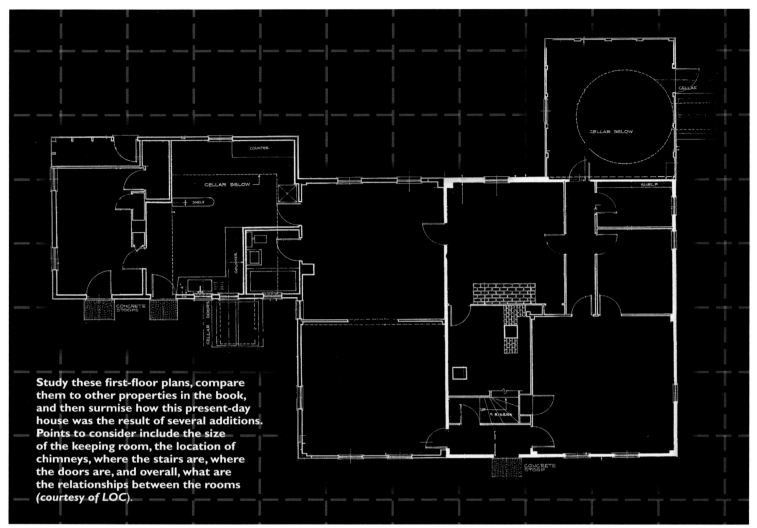

Study these first-floor plans, compare them to other properties in the book, and then surmise how this present-day house was the result of several additions. Points to consider include the size of the keeping room, the location of chimneys, where the stairs are, where the doors are, and overall, what are the relationships between the rooms (courtesy of LOC).

This image from the 1960 HABS survey shows what is now the bedroom behind the door seen in the previous image.

A present-day image of the area directly behind the front door. Note the wide-board wall; directly behind it are the stairs to the second floor. The door in the background opens to a bedroom.

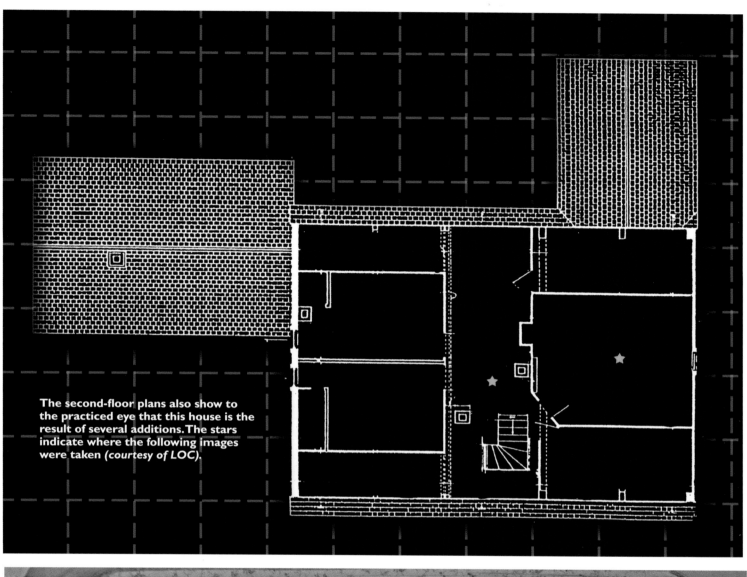

The second-floor plans also show to the practiced eye that this house is the result of several additions. The stars indicate where the following images were taken *(courtesy of LOC)*.

A view of the largest bedroom on the second floor, which is no longer used as a living space. This view of the room shows the stairs (left); the fireplace, which once had a stove in it but is no longer functional; and a small closet.

Two present-day views of the roof and the chimney, which has been repaired. Note that the purlins are not continuous, indicating an addition.

Isaac Smith House, 1738
Eastham, Massachusetts

Drive to the other side of Eastham and on a back road is another full Cape house, which is reputed to be one of the oldest in the town. As is typical of a house built more than two hundred and seventy years ago in a rural, agricultural locale, the trim is plain, there is a central entry with a five-light transom, and six over six windows that are at least a century old. Family records indicate a definitive line of ownership that accurately dates when the house was constructed. It is interesting to note that the daughter of the original owner married Ephraim Harding from Truro, who may have been related to the next property described in the following pages. In the accompanying images, several additions can be seen that were added to the rear and west side of the house. Well maintained, this dwelling is an excellent example of the Cape Cod house architectural style.

The front door with the original rock step.

The west side of the house with several additions, including the porch in the foreground.

Facing south, the Isaac Smith house illustrates its vintage with windows directly under the roof-line. Compare images of this house with the previous Doane house and the next Harding house.

ISAAC SMITH HOUSE
1738

Lot Harding House, 1746-1775
Truro, Massachusetts

While it is not the intent of this book to find the oldest house in any community on the Cape, the HABS survey of 1959-60, after extensive examination and attention to details of the property, determined that this building may be the oldest in Truro. It has also been compared to the Sylvanus Doane House in Eastham, which is pictured on previous pages. While the exact date of construction cannot be specified, information from family records, maps, and historical documents indicates that the house was built between 1746 and 1775. The house, timber framed with vertical plank construction and facing south, is a traditional five-bay, center chimney with one and a half stories. The dimensions, thirty-nine feet by thirty-one feet, are slightly larger than the typical full Cape. Since the survey was completed fifty years ago, several renovations have taken place, including the installation of more modern windows. Compare the images to note the differences. The previous owner used the property as a summer residence; it is now occupied year round. There are two cellars, each made of brick and about twelve feet in diameter, accessed through the bulkhead and doghouse that can be seen in the photographs.

This old family photograph is of the Lot Harding House previous to the hurricane of 193

Compare these two sets of images of the front and rear of the house and note the changes that have occurred in the last fifty years. The large window on the rear wall is found in the keeping room; the street is about one hundred yards to the north (*black and white courtesy of LOC*).

Two views of the west side of the house; besides the distinctive architectural changes, a modern day satellite television dish can be found near the peak (*black and white courtesy of LOC*).

The east side of the house.

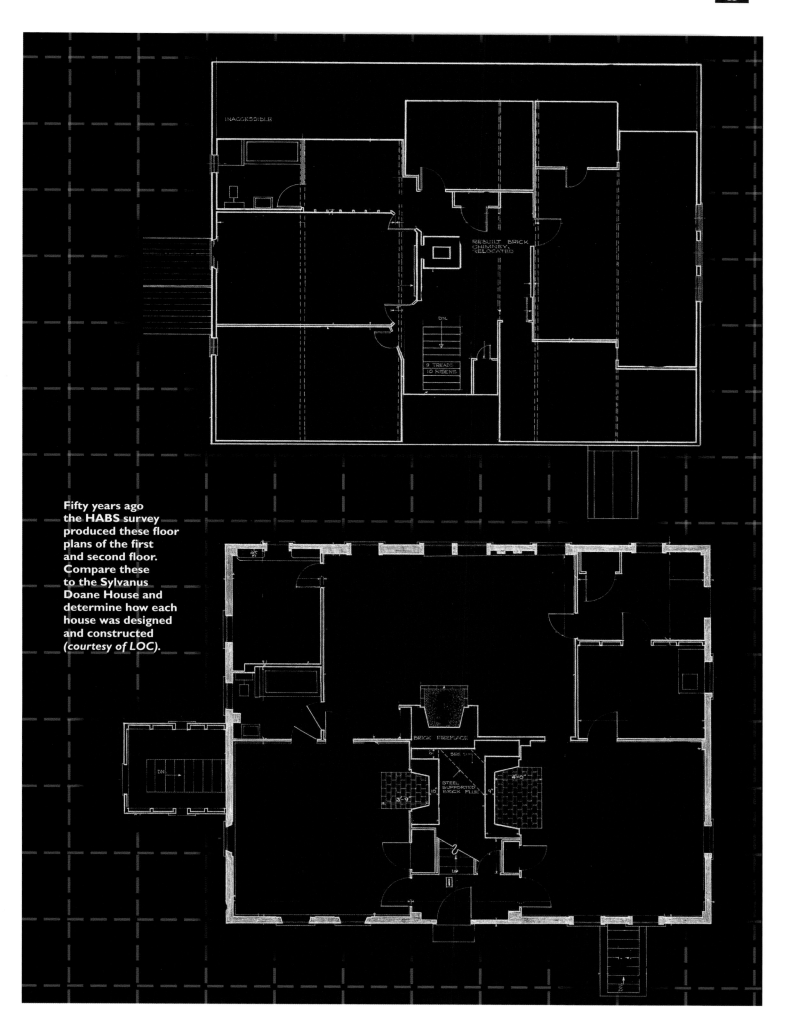

Fifty years ago the HABS survey produced these floor plans of the first and second floor. Compare these to the Sylvanus Doane House and determine how each house was designed and constructed *(courtesy of LOC).*

INACCESSIBLE

REBUILT BRICK CHIMNEY, RELOCATED

DN.

9 TREADS
10 RISERS

BRICK FIREPLACE

STEEL SUPPORTED BRICK FLUE

DN.

UP

Using the first-floor plans, identify the location of the three fireplaces, all functional, in these sets of images taken fifty years apart. Note the paneling, cupboards, and woodwork in each of the rooms (*black and white courtesy of LOC*).

Emory Welles House, 1820
Wellfleet, Massachusetts

After examining the interiors of the other houses illustrated on these pages, it becomes obvious that the Welles house is architecturally significant in that so little has been changed. The original first-floor plan is intact. A buttery, two small bedrooms, and a back staircase are found off the keeping room, which has been converted to a dining room. An addition to the rear now houses the modern kitchen. There is a small round cellar and the entire house has a low brick foundation. The front door has a leaded fanlight which also has two over two sidelights.

THIS PROPERTY HAS BEEN PLACED ON THE NATIONAL REGISTER OF HISTORIC PLACES BY THE UNITED STATES DEPARTMENT OF THE INTERIOR BUILT 1820

This federal full Cape, built in 1820, has been listed on the National Register of Historic Places.

The front door features a fan light above and side lights on either side. Note the original nine over six panes in the windows.

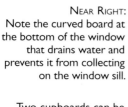

The east side of the house. The addition to the right has a modern kitchen.

NEAR RIGHT: Note the curved board at the bottom of the window that drains water and prevents it from collecting on the window sill.

Two cupboards can be found in the keeping room, where the fireplace is still functional. The door to the left leads to the parlor; the front door is in the background.

FAR RIGHT: There are no nails or screws in the front door. The panels are held together with pegs, seen here just above the red lines.

The parlor is the front southeast room in the house.

Narrow stairs from the second floor lead towards the front door.

From the modern kitchen, the original back door leads to the keeping room.

There are two bedrooms on the second floor; this is the one on the east side of the house.

Doane Houses
Eighteenth Century
Eastham, Massachusetts

The following two Doane houses (there are several other Doane Houses identified in this book), built in the late 1700s, are well maintained and exquisite examples of this down-to-earth architectural house style. Uniquely, they both face west instead of south. They also show the effort owners have undertaken to preserve their properties. This may not have been true sixty-five years ago. The population increase on the Outer Cape, due to tourism and second homes, didn't begin until after WWII. Before that, many of the older houses, as well as the outbuildings, fell into disrepair and were torn down. Sometimes, the wood beams and lumber would be used in other houses. At least one of these houses, the half Cape illustrated here, was in serious need of repair. When the chimney falls through the roof, it's time to make some significant repairs. Charred wood on the inside of the house next to the chimney indicated the distinct possibility that a fire could have destroyed this historic home. Improvements have been made to both of these houses to allow easier livability; changes have been made, such as window replacement, but all retain their historic fabric. Located within the Cape Cod National Seashore, these two houses are protected from being torn down so a bigger, newer structure could be built. Each house is now used primarily as a summer residence.

Taken more than fifty years apart, these two images show a basic half Cape: the Simeon Doane house. One of the many difficulties researchers have in identifying properties by looking at town maps is the absence of a first name. Mostly, the map would use the first initial. In this case, there happened to be a Simeon, Solomon, and Sylvanus Doane, all living within a short distance of each other in Eastham. The date of original construction is difficult to determine in part because the house may have been moved to this location and has had several subsequent additions. Historians suggest it may have been built in the early to mid-1700s. Many of these original houses had only a root cellar (about ten feet in diameter) that was accessed through a small addition (doghouse). Improvements to this house include a cellar, which can be reached through the bulkhead. Electricity, heat, and telephone were not installed in the house until 1955. A nearby shed may have been a two-hole outhouse that was in use until the early 1960s.

The bow-roof can be seen in this view. Building a house with a bow-roof took more time, both in planning and in construction, as the roof rafters would have to be shaped. The rafters would be supported at a point, somewhere near the middle, and weights put on each end to bend the beams. The beams could take up to a year to be ready for construction.

A previous owner used this property, which is only a short distance from the local marsh—a renowned stopover during the fall bird migrations—as a hunting camp. The ell to the rear increases the size of this Cape. Notice the arrangement of the doors.

This second nearby Doane house, a full Cape within the National Seashore, shows signs of Greek Revival influence on the front door. Four windows, two large and two small, are typical of a full Cape. Also, there is the distinctive ell to the back of the house.

Bourn House
Eighteenth Century
Wellfleet, Massachusetts

Compare this house to the Doane houses in Eastham (page 54) and notice the similarities. That's because this is a Doane house, built sometime around 1750, in what is now Wellfleet. When new owners acquire a property, renovations and improvements are made to upgrade the livability of the house. Sometimes when these changes are made, past structural details are discovered. In this house, it was revealed that in the walls, instead of studs, small trees with branches still attached, provided support. This may have been a common construction feature found in these early houses. Unfortunately, no visual evidence remains of this remodeling. Hidden amongst the trees and tucked in among houses on a side street, this south-facing bow-roofed three-quarter Cape is found in the lee of a hill to the north. Two indicators of the age of the house are the windows that are tucked up under the relatively short eaves and the narrow window trim. The shorter the overhang, the less damage the winter winds could cause.

The bow-roof, not distinctively apparent when you first look at the house, has a similar roof-line to houses in Eastham. Compare also the number and arrangement of windows on the second floor. Obviously, the small sizes of the windows indicate an early construction date. The ornamental trim on the windows is an added feature.

Two views showing the front, left, and right sides of the house that has five outside doors. Three can be seen in these images. Historical examination has determined that some of the hardware in the house is original. There are six fireplaces on the first floor and only one on the second floor. Each wall with a fireplace is totally wood, consisting of paneling and doors. All other walls have a chair rail with a wood panel below. The fireplace in the keeping room has a beehive oven. "Good Morning" stairs lead to a bedroom and a sitting room. Indian shutters are built into frames of the windows.

Captain Beniah Gill, 1730
Eastham, Massachusetts

This three-quarter Cape, like many others in Eastham, has its original sparse detail plus several modern additions to increase the living space. Originally located further west, next to several cranberry bogs, and closer to outer Wellfleet Harbor, the house was moved to its present position near a road at some unknown date. Some of the original wainscoting remains in the house, but many features, including fireplaces, no longer exist. Renovations and modernization have resulted in a very comfortable home. A year-round residence for many years, the house was a favorite with photographers; now it is primarily a summer home.

Taken fifty or more years apart, and with flowers in bloom, the Gill House is still a favorite of photographers. Structurally, little has changed about the house. Note the lack of details in the different trim locations.

Compare this bow-roof to the previous house and notice the similarity. A breezeway and garage have been added to the north side of the house.

An entry way addition is found attached to the south side of the house. On the second floor, there is only one window on this side.

Shadrack Standish House, 1730
Halifax, Massachusetts

A little more than ten miles from where the Pilgrims landed in Plymouth, Halifax is now a rural agricultural community with numerous older, well-preserved homes. One of the properties surveyed by the HABS in 1934 was this full Cape, the Shadrack Standish House. Nearly eighty years ago, the house, which faces east and a nearby road, was in need of repair; now it is a well-maintained home.

Two views of the Standish House, captured eighty years apart.

HABS plans and elevations for this thirty-eight by thirty full Cape

This image of the parlor was captured in the early 1930s; find its location on the plans. The door to the right leads to the keeping room (*courtesy of LOC*).

The keeping room with the typical beehive oven (*courtesy of LOC*).

Josiah Higgins, 1830
Wellfleet, Massachusetts

Sitting on a hill overlooking the ponds in Wellfleet, this image from the 1920s shows the Josiah Higgins house and its neighbors in the background. One of the nearby ponds, Higgins, was supposedly named after the original owner of the home (*courtesy of WHS*).

Originally built and owned by Josiah Higgins, this Georgian Cape house, located within the boundaries of the Cape Cod National Seashore, has now been owned by the same family for more than one hundred years—its history is well documented. While the earliest house may have been built sometime between 1750 and 1765, windows and interior moldings indicate a date of construction in the early 1800s. But those improvements might have been renovations after the house had been built. Unlike many other Capes, this Cape has never been moved. Now a year-round residence, the house has had several renovations and modernizations for interior plumbing and an efficient kitchen, yet still retains the fabric of a dwelling built more than a century and a half ago.

Salty Dog relaxes in front of the house on a sunny summer day.

The framing in the roof can be seen in this second-floor bedroom. Note the random-width boards that make up the roof.

The front southeast room has a cupboard and two windows that look out on a local pond.

Two opposing views of the front door. Narrow stairs behind the door lead to the second floor; the house cat, not allowed outside, sits within two V-shaped boards that collect rain water from under the door and drain it through an opening. Note the random-width floor boards.

The two front rooms can be seen on each side of the still-functional keeping room fireplace.

Gambrels

Any discussion of the architectural style that is the Cape house must also include the variation that involves the distinctive two-sided roofline. Most commonly known as Dutch gambrel, this roof-line adds more head space on the second floor. Part of the Dutch language as early as 1600, the "gambrill" was defined as a crooked stick and not only referred to the roof-line discussed here but also to the hind legs of a slaughtered animal. Originally discovered by European explorers to Southeast Asia, and particularly Indonesia, the two-sided roof was used by the natives in a variety of dwellings. It was brought back to Europe, where it was adapted in different countries for local conditions. It was then brought to America, where the colonists, along the east coast, built gambrel roofs that varied according to the length and slopes of the two roofs. Since various European settlers had distinctive roofline designs that are relatively easy to recognize, historical architects are able to distinguish regional variations such as Swedish or Dutch, among others. It is important to note that the front and rear rooflines are always nearly identical, this can be observed in a side view. Another factor that makes this roofline more advantageous is that the lumber required to construct the roof frame need not be as long as the traditional straight-sloped roof. Even though the gambrels described here are some of the oldest identified houses in this book, it is a relatively rare house style on Cape Cod and extremely rare on the Outer Cape.

The image of the house and the plan, although different buildings, both show the distinctive gambrel style roofline. By having a joint or break in the roof, more space is added to the second floor. Depending on the regions of the country where they were built, the angle and length of each section would vary. Note the variation in rooflines in the following pages (*courtesy of LOC*).

Described here, the Jonathan Atwood House in Chatham, which has gambrels, is a museum and headquarters for the Chatham Historical Society. More common in the area around Plymouth, several gambrels have been examined. Compare the floor plans of these gambrels to the plans of several full Capes illustrated throughout the book and note the similarity.

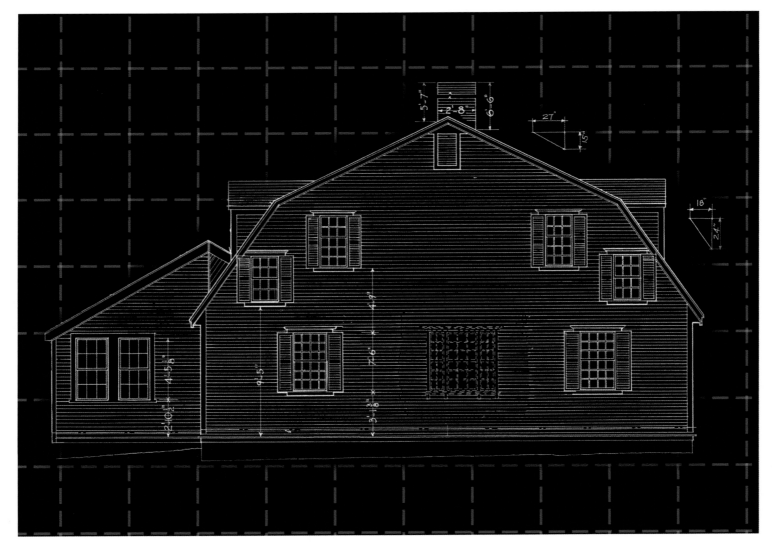

Samuel Lincoln House, 1650
Hingham, Massachusetts

Built more than three and a half centuries ago, the Samuel Lincoln house in Hingham is one the oldest extant houses described in this book. Well maintained by the Hingham Historical Society, this house was part of the HABS examination more than a half-century ago. Samuel immigrated to America in 1637 and settled in Hingham. One of his sons and grandson moved to Pennsylvania. Four generations later, on February 12, 1809, was born a son, Abraham, who would become the sixteenth President of the United States.

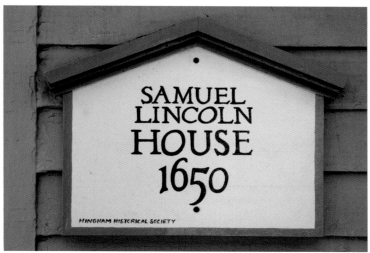

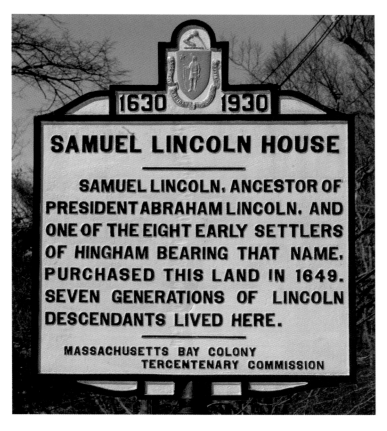

Located on a busy street near Hingham Harbor, the Samuel Lincoln house has a distinctive gambrel roof.

Maintained by the Hingham Historical Society, the house has a front view that is typical of a full Cape. In a nearby park is a statue of Abraham Lincoln, the sixth great-grandson of the original owner of this house.

The five-plank front door.

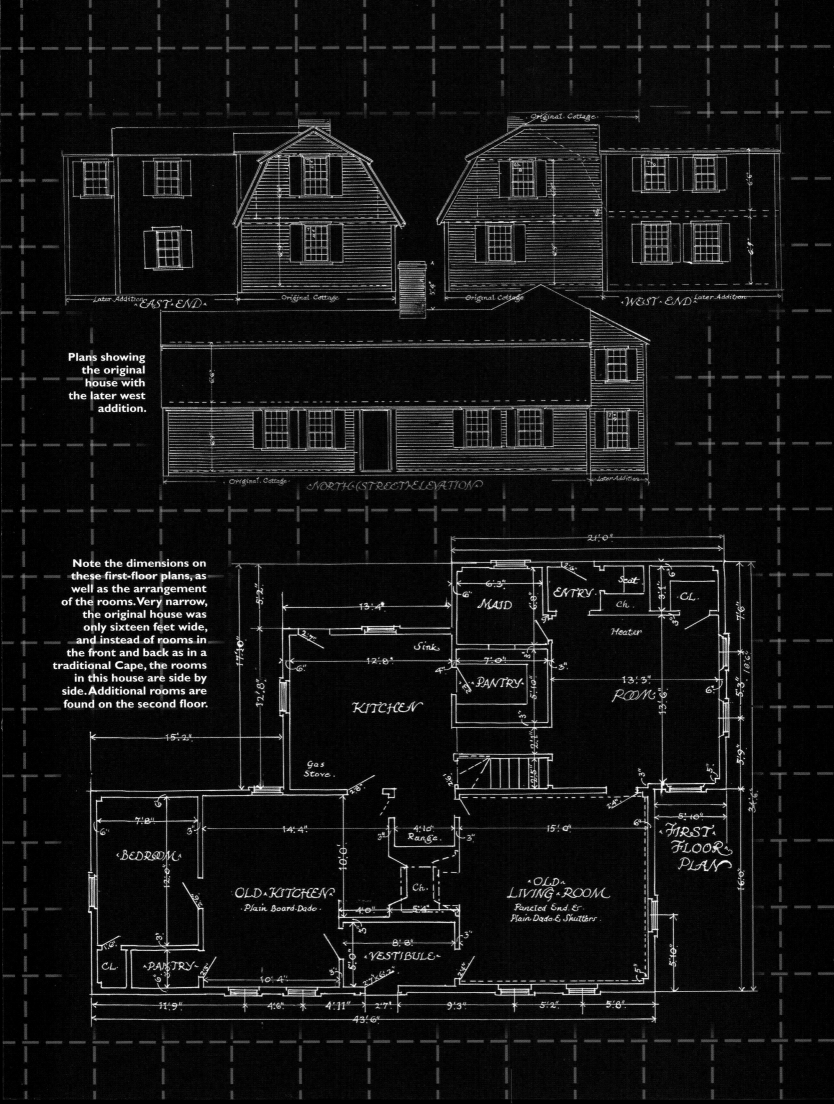

EAST·END· Later Addition · Original Cottage

WEST·END· Original Cottage · Later Addition

NORTH·(STREET)·ELEVATION · Original·Cottage · Later Addition

Plans showing the original house with the later west addition.

Note the dimensions on these first-floor plans, as well as the arrangement of the rooms. Very narrow, the original house was only sixteen feet wide, and instead of rooms in the front and back as in a traditional Cape, the rooms in this house are side by side. Additional rooms are found on the second floor.

MAID

ENTRY

Seat

CL.

Ch.

Heater

KITCHEN

Sink

PANTRY

ROOM

Gas Stove.

·FIRST· ·FLOOR· ·PLAN·

·OLD·KITCHEN· ·Plain·Board·Dado·

Range.

Ch.

·OLD· ·LIVING·ROOM· ·Paneled·End·&· ·Plain·Dado·&·Shutters·

·BEDROOM·

·VESTIBULE·

CL.

·PANTRY·

Original Cottage

The house has only one window for each floor because it is so narrow. Note in the plans that the first-floor ceiling is 6'9" and the second floor, because of the roof-line, is 6'6".

A view of the west side with the later addition to the rear.

Pilgrim Cottage, 1687
Hingham, Massachusetts

The second of the two oldest houses found in this book, the Pilgrim Cottage is also unique in that it has a gambrel roof. Compare this roofline to the previously mentioned Samuel Lincoln house and observe that they are probably the same. The Lincoln house is about two miles away and closer to the harbor.

The front stairs and the small historical sign.

Two images of this gambrel taken almost eighty years apart. An addition to the rear, air conditioning, and an exterior electric meter are the changes that have occurred since then. Note the stone foundation and the wood-shingled roof.

Tucked between larger homes on this tree-lined road that leads to Hingham center is the Pilgrim Cottage, which is now a private residence.

William Harlow House, 1677
Plymouth, Massachusetts

One of the oldest, 1677, and best-preserved gambrels is the William Harlow House in Plymouth, Massachusetts. A farmer and a soldier, Sergeant William Harlow was given permission to use materials from the fort on nearby Burial Hill when it was torn down after King Philip's War. Hand-hewn beams and wide-planked floors almost four hundred years old can be seen in this old house. Purchased in 1920 by the Plymouth Antiquarian Society, this one-and-a-half- story house, with a large central fireplace and chimney, has been restored and preserved to show daily life in seventeenth-century New England. Now a museum, the house is open during the summer season and contains early artifacts and costumed interpreters to demonstrate colonial crafts. Facing south, the house is located on a street that used to be the main road between Plymouth and Sandwich.

This century-old postcard of the Harlow residence was taken when the house was still a private residence. Compare it to the present-day color image of the house that has been restored and maintained to pristine condition.

John And Sarah Guild, 1714
Wrentham, Massachusetts

As mentioned in the author's notes, houses were selected to be included in this book from two sources. The first resource was houses that had been examined by the Massachusetts Historical Commission and their reports on file at either (or both) the local community library or historical society. A second and more detailed source of information that includes plans and photographs is the Historic American Building Survey that is part of the Library of Congress collection and website. The Guild House was part of the HABS assessment that was completed more than seventy years ago. Part of my recent research into this property also determined that this house is a First Order dwelling. By definition, a First Order house was built between 1620 and 1720 and has been researched and recognized by the Plymouth Antiquarian Society (PAS). Throughout the South Shore, properties have been identified, including the Guild House, which are of architectural significance. Located in Plymouth, Massachusetts, the PAS has three properties that it maintains; the oldest is the 1677 Harlow House, which also happens to be a gambrel roof structure.

The first owner of this acreage in Wrentham was John Guild, a Dedham resident who was given the property as a land grant in 1676. His son, also John, inherited the property from his father in 1682 and built a simple house with one room over another room. Documents exist from the "Great and General Court" which encouraged the building of houses by offering "Bills of Credit" to existing homesteads; one property included in these documents was this house owned by Sarah and John Guild. A recent owner has spent time restoring the interior to its previous condition, including its original fireplaces, ceiling beams, wainscoting, and where possible, restoration quality hardware and accents. A possible explanation of why this property is still standing when so many were burned during the uprisings with the Native Americans is that white flags were hung on the house to indicate disease (possibly smallpox). For that reason, the house would be avoided. Now, the Guild House is an excellent example of a house built almost three centuries ago.

These two views of the house were taken more than seventy years apart. Because the house was a rental property for many years, very few drastic changes or major renovations have been completed; the house has maintained the flavor of its original character. Located on a busy thoroughfare, it is possible to see the road in the black and white image. A sign, with the assistance of the Wrentham Historical Commission, dates the construction of the earliest house on the property (*black and white courtesy of LOC*).

Except for the entry addition, the west side of the house is a mirror image of the east side. In many traditional Capes, the windows on each side of the house are usually different in number and size.

The distinctive gambrel roofline can be seen in this photograph of the east side of the house. An inside view from the front window on the second floor can be seen in a following image.

The following series of paired images show the same view taken more than seventy-five years apart. The black and white photographs were captured in 1936 by a HABS photographer and are used with the permission of the Library of Congress. The first pair of images shows the front door.

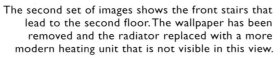

The second set of images shows the front stairs that lead to the second floor. The wallpaper has been removed and the radiator replaced with a more modern heating unit that is not visible in this view.

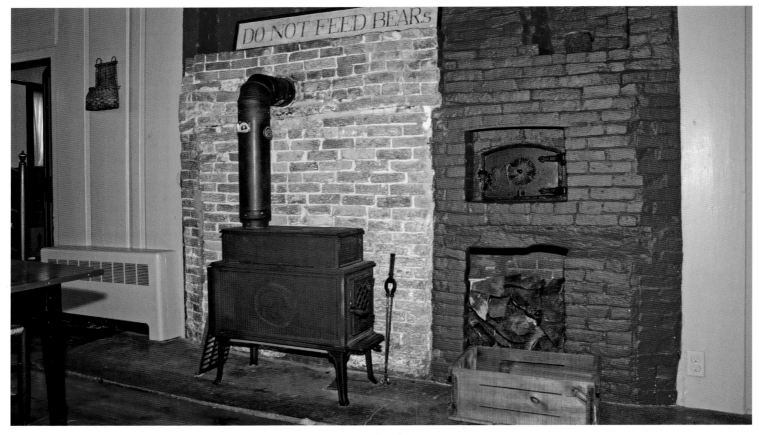

The two views of the keeping room show drastic differences that have occurred through the years. The beehive oven is no longer functional and a wood burning stove has replaced the bricked-up fireplace.

Behind the front stairs, it is possible to see the original chimney with the bulbous beehive oven.

Despite being taken years apart, the front southeast room is easily recognizable in these images.

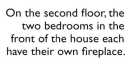

On the second floor, the two bedrooms in the front of the house each have their own fireplace.

A four-poster bed occupies the room with the window on the east side of the house.

At the rear of the second floor, space has been converted to a modern bathroom; roof rafters can also be seen.

Joseph Atwood House, 1752
Chatham, Massachusetts

The oldest house in Chatham, on the road to Stage Harbor, was built about 1752, when a Colonel Elisha Doane of Eastham sold roughly thirty acres to Joseph Atwood. A sea captain, Atwood built the house between voyages. The house remained in the Atwood family until 1926, when it was bequeathed to the Chatham Historical Society. Unusual for its gambrel roof, which is rare on the Outer Cape, this house, now a museum, is a superb example of a house that is more than two and half centuries old.

Three images of the Joseph Atwood House taken over a span of one hundred years.

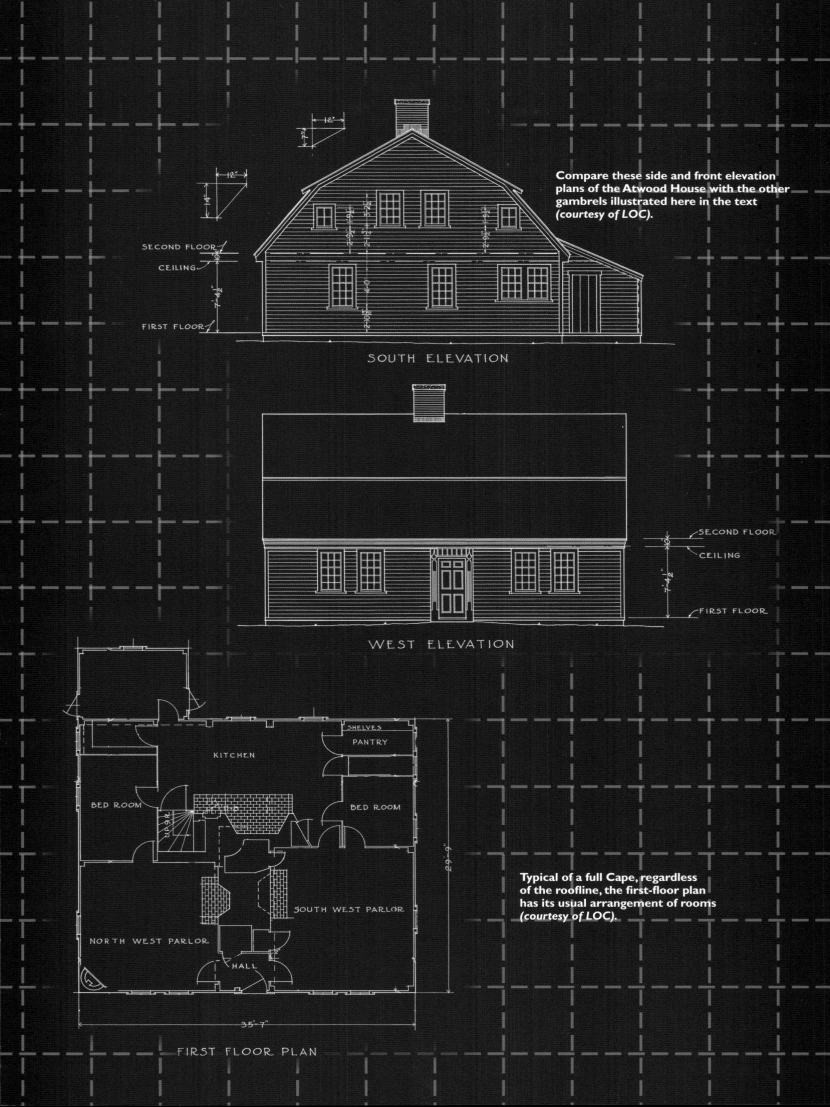

SOUTH ELEVATION

SECOND FLOOR

CEILING

FIRST FLOOR

Compare these side and front elevation plans of the Atwood House with the other gambrels illustrated here in the text *(courtesy of LOC).*

WEST ELEVATION

SECOND FLOOR

CEILING

FIRST FLOOR

KITCHEN

SHELVES

PANTRY

BED ROOM

BED ROOM

NORTH WEST PARLOR

SOUTH WEST PARLOR

HALL

FIRST FLOOR PLAN

Typical of a full Cape, regardless of the roofline, the first-floor plan has its usual arrangement of rooms *(courtesy of LOC).*

Two scenes of the first floor of the Atwood House taken during a HABS examination: the keeping room, with stairs leading to the second floor, and an unusual corner cupboard (*courtesy of LOC*).

Sproat-Ward House, c. 1712
Lakeville, Massachusetts

Travel the back roads west of Plymouth, and although traditional old Capes maybe more common, there are also classic antique gambrels that may even be older. The Sproat-Ward House in Lakeville, hidden on a treed street, has a history; the home of a Revolutionary War general, it has secret rooms, and openings that allowed inhabitants to fire on unfriendlies. Several additions have been made to the rear of the house through the years.

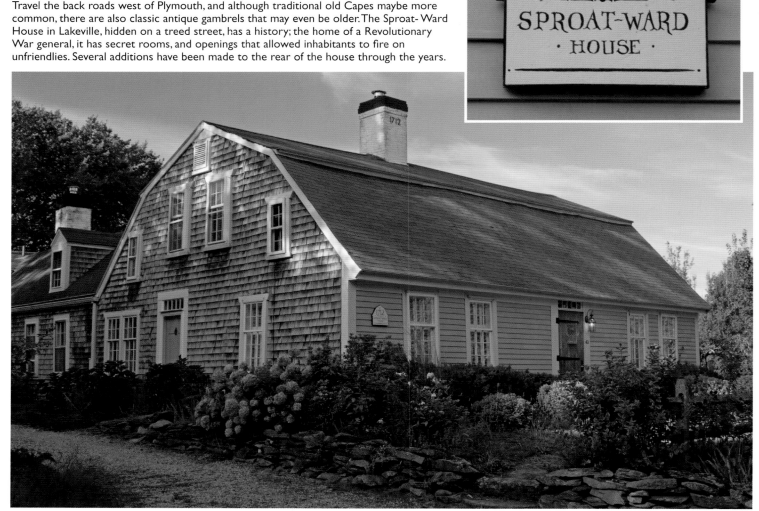

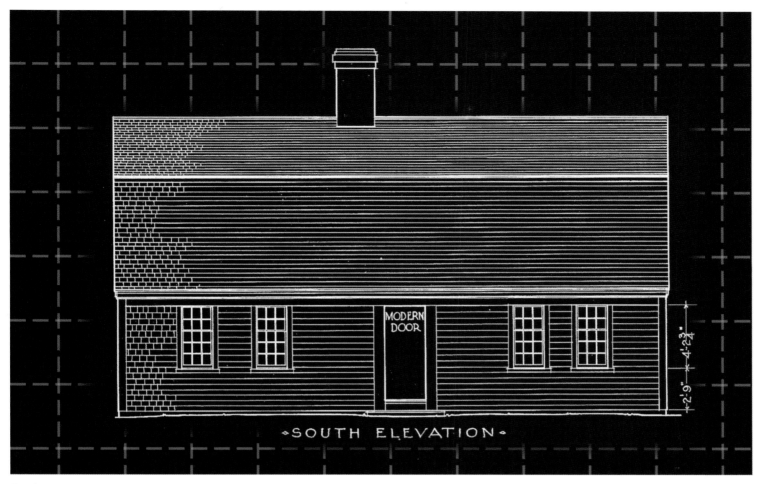

◆SOUTH ELEVATION◆

The Sproat-Ward House faces south in this front elevation view (*courtesy of LOC*).

The front door of the house with restoration hardware added since the HABS image (opposite and bottom; *courtesy of LOC*) was captured seventy years ago..

An image and HABS plans of the west side of the house (*plan courtesy of LOC*).

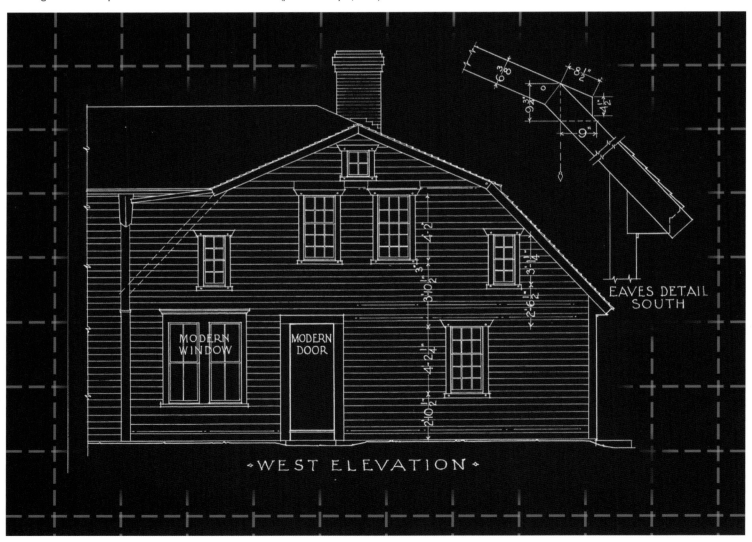

EAVES DETAIL
SOUTH

MODERN
WINDOW

MODERN
DOOR

◆ WEST ELEVATION ◆

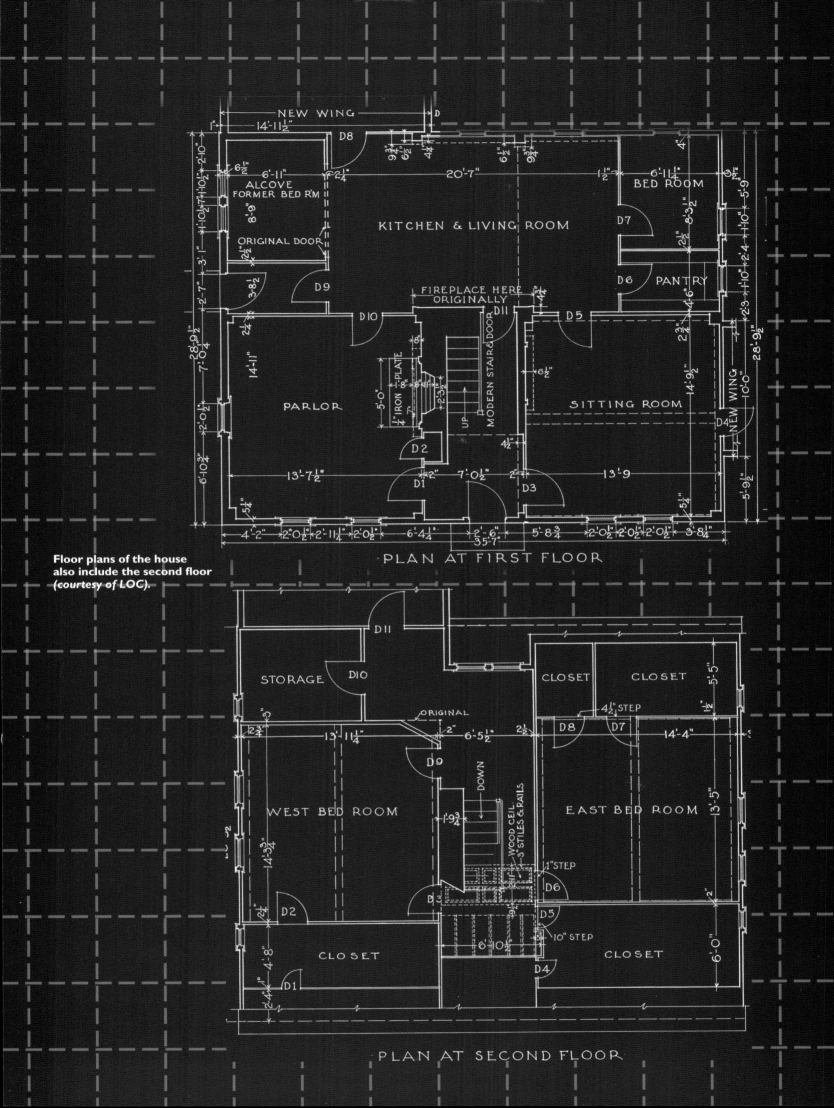

Floor plans of the house also include the second floor (courtesy of LOC).

PLAN AT FIRST FLOOR

NEW WING
14'-11½"

ALCOVE
FORMER BED R'M

KITCHEN & LIVING ROOM

BED ROOM

ORIGINAL DOOR

PANTRY

FIREPLACE HERE
ORIGINALLY

PARLOR

SITTING ROOM

NEW WING

PLAN AT SECOND FLOOR

STORAGE

CLOSET   CLOSET

ORIGINAL

WEST BED ROOM

EAST BED ROOM

CLOSET

CLOSET

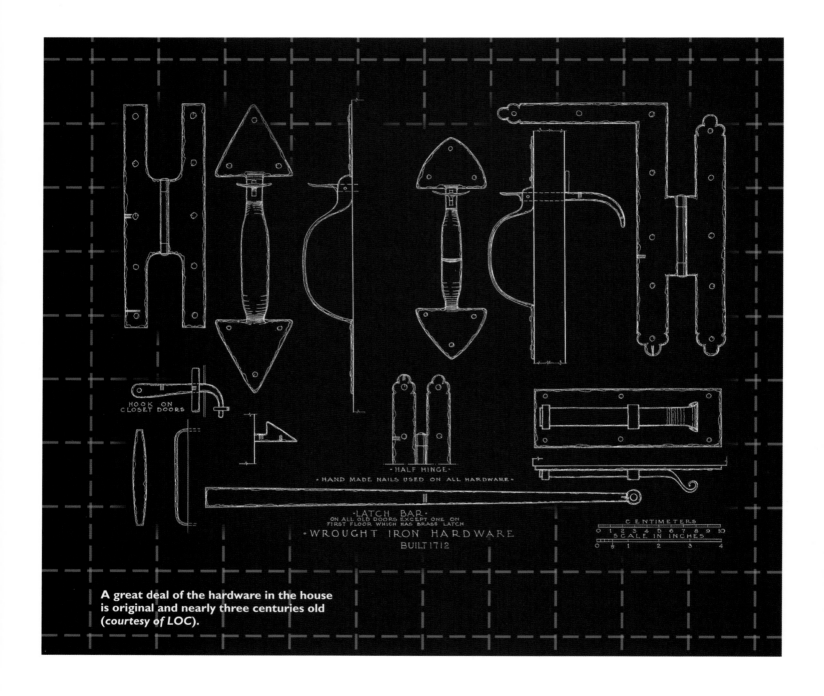

HOOK ON CLOSET DOORS

·HALF HINGE·
· HAND MADE NAILS USED ON ALL HARDWARE ·

·LATCH BAR·
ON ALL OLD DOORS EXCEPT ONE ON
FIRST FLOOR WHICH HAS BRASS LATCH
·WROUGHT IRON HARDWARE
BUILT 1712

CENTIMETERS
0 1 2 3 4 5 6 7 8 9 10
SCALE IN INCHES
0 1 2 3 4

A great deal of the hardware in the house is original and nearly three centuries old (*courtesy of LOC*).

The front of this five-bay house gives no indication of the roofline.

Located in nearby Marshfield, the Ford House, with its gambrel roof, was moved to this location from where it was originally built near Plymouth Rock.

The parlor, located in the right front of the house, has a fireplace and two cupboards.

In nearby Kingston is this center-chimney gambrel built in 1754.

Crosby Mansion
Early 1800s
Brewster, Massachusetts

So what happens when you just can't leave the house you were born in? You build your mansion around it! Albert Crosby, born in 1823, was raised in this full Cape that had been built in the early 1800s. A businessman, Albert was first involved in maritime trade between Boston and the West Indies. He then moved to Chicago where he became extremely wealthy selling medicinal alcohol during the Civil War. After divorcing his first wife, he married Matilda, twenty years younger, and honeymooned in Europe for more than a decade. When he returned to Brewster, a "summer home" was built that included thirty-five rooms and seventeen fireplaces. No expense was spared with the use of imported tiles, marble sinks, and floors, as well as an impressive collection of paintings and statuary. The mansion was completed in 1888 and named Tawasentha. Helen Keller and Mark Twain were just some of the visitors. Albert, it was said, when he tired of the mansion, would retire to his home within a home. Now in the process of restoration, the mansion has been furnished with period pieces and is open for weddings and special events, as well as tours during the summer season.

A second view of the full Cape, with the mansion that was built around it. The door on the side of the house allowed servants who lived nearby to enter and leave the house and then the mansion.

The red front door leads into the house; the back door enters the keeping room from the mansion.

A partial view of the front of the mansion. Compare the chimneys to the original Cape house picture.

Two images of the bedroom. The maroon door was seen in a previous image; the bright red door in the background leads to the servant's quarters.

These two views are of the keeping room; it is possible to look through the doors and see the other rooms.

There are two rooms in the front of the house; this is the living room.

These two images are of the other front room, the parlor.

Joseph N. Howe, 1830
Milton, Massachusetts

Most early Cape-style houses were built from lumber harvested in nearby woods, or as on the Outer Cape, debris collected from shipwrecks. This one-and-a-half-story Cape in Milton, Massachusetts, was built by Joseph N. Howe in 1830 of granite from the local quarries. The house is well documented and its history is known from public records.

These two black and white images were taken in 1936 by the photographer Arthur C. Haskell as part of the Library of Congress' HABS. They show the front of the house and the east-facing end. Notice that there is now a window where the front door used to be located. This renovation may have been completed by a previous owner because the house faces a very busy street. A driveway now circles the property, allowing the main entrance to be in the back of the house (*courtesy of LOC*).

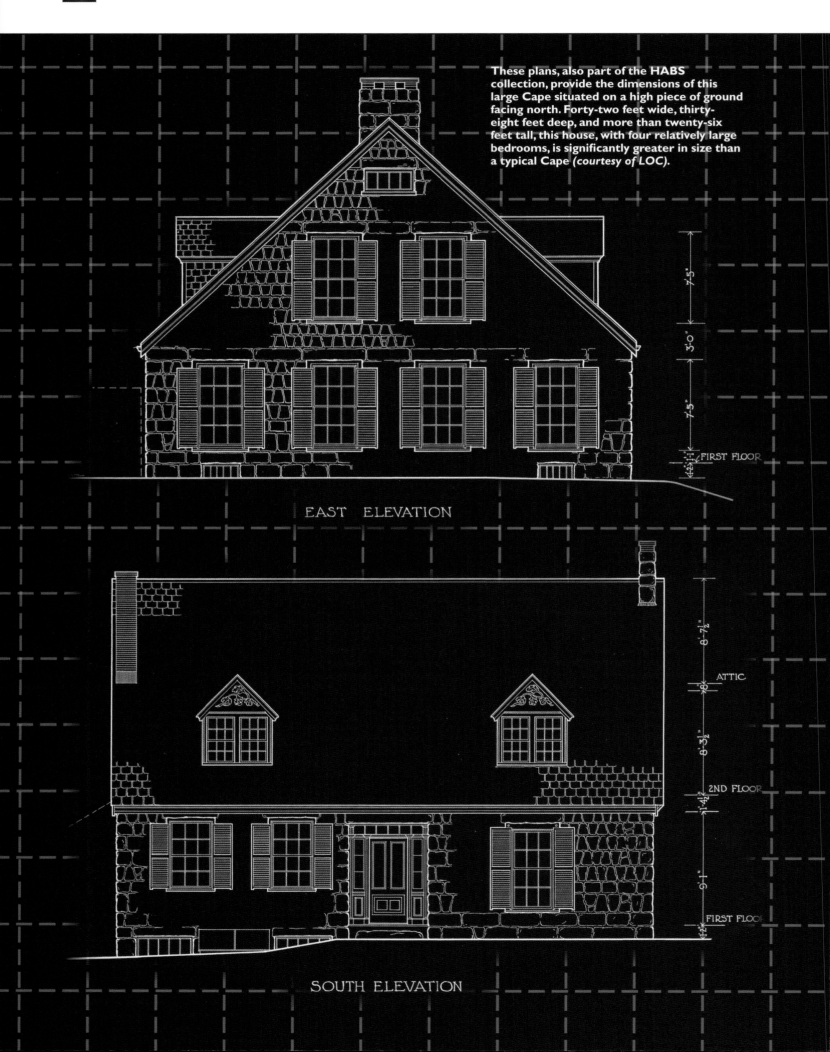

These plans, also part of the **HABS** collection, provide the dimensions of this large **Cape** situated on a high piece of ground facing north. Forty-two feet wide, thirty-eight feet deep, and more than twenty-six feet tall, this house, with four relatively large bedrooms, is significantly greater in size than a typical **Cape** *(courtesy of LOC).*

EAST ELEVATION

SOUTH ELEVATION

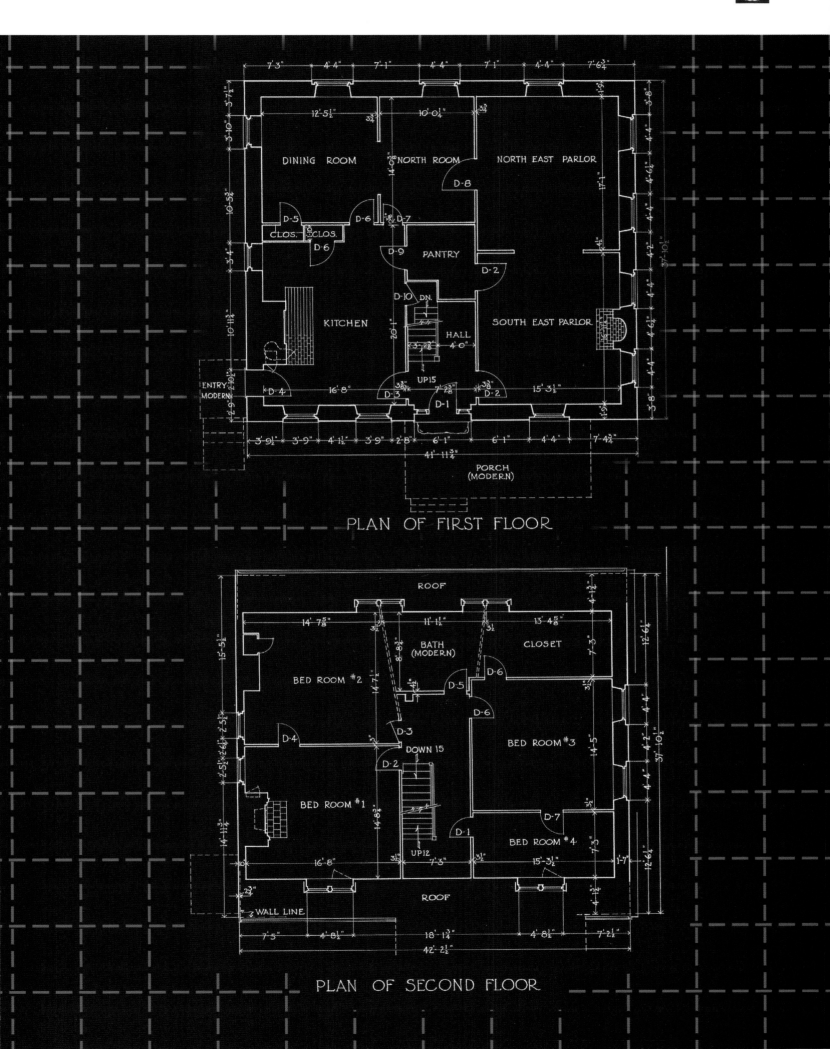

PLAN OF FIRST FLOOR

PLAN OF SECOND FLOOR

A modern-day view of the east end of the house, which is now part of a religious organization. Two large shed roofs have been added to the front and back to provide additional living space on the second floor.

Closer examination of the east end of the house shows the arrangement of the unique triangular granite blocks that were used in construction. Examine the other images to observe that the other walls have the same pattern of triangular granite blocks.

Jenkins House, 1700
Barnstable, Massachusetts

Most of the properties illustrated and examined in this book are just a house and in some cases there may also be a barn. Years ago, the property may have been about twenty, thirty, or forty acres with a house, a barn for a variety of animals, and probably several other out buildings. More than a century later, the Jenkins farm in Barnstable is reminiscent of what a typical Cape Cod farm would have been like.

When viewing this property, if one saw this white half Cape and assumed it was the oldest, one would be mistaken. The half Cape was built in 1840; the ell to the rear was added n 1852. Also on the property is this small cottage that may have been built as early as 1700.

The large barn that once housed cows and sheep was built in 1895 for $500.

Two views of the east side of the house.

Looking east, stone walls built more than a century ago mark fields where animals used to graze.

A view of the back of the property, which includes a barn and several outbuildings. The white chimney in the center is the main house.

The farm no longer raises animals; since 1870 they have maintained numerous acres of cranberry bogs.

Other Capes

Centuries ago houses were built along the main thoroughfares when stagecoaches and horse drawn wagons were the usual form of transportation; now those roads are highways with fast and continuous traffic. This is probably not the most advantageous place to live. Today, some of these Capes have been remodeled and modernized and are active business locations. The following four properties are examples of one-time residences that have been altered yet are still easily recognizable as Capes.

Now housing a gift shop, this two-century-old Cape is located on a busy highway in North Eastham. With some parts that may be as old as the seventeenth century, this house (never moved), at one time was a stop on the stagecoach line, a post office, and a hotel with an ice skating rink; it is now a gift shop as part of a plant nursery. Recognizable changes include the removal of the center chimney and the addition of modern windows.

Two views of the front room with its original wide-planked floors and framing.

A close-up of a framing joint. The angled piece in the front is not original and has been added to provide support. Note the carved initials, "BN," which may be centuries old.

A view of the north gable end of the house.

Beetles, probably powderpost beetles, have attacked these floorboards. Note the traces of gray paint that remain after the floor was returned to original condition.

Originally built on Billingsgate Island about two hundred years ago, this three-quarter Cape was moved more than a century ago when the land, washed away by winter storms, started to disappear. Several other homes on nearby streets were also moved from the island. In Wellfleet, this house is now a fine dining restaurant.

Two views of the front parlor room.

Some of the original walls
have been removed from
inside the house; floorboards
indicate where different
rooms may have been.

The keeping room
fireplace with
original paneling.

Brightly colored and modernized, the Eliphalet Edson House, now located on the King's Highway in Yarmouth, is another fine dining restaurant.

This dining room is at the front of the house.

This black and white was captured as part of a HABS exam fifty years ago, when the Cape Cod National Seashore was in its formative stages. Known as the "bog house" and located in North Truro, this full Cape was expanded not by raising the roof, but by lifting the house and placing another floor on ground level. Why? The owners at the time had several cranberry bogs and the first level was used in that endeavor.

These three views show the different sides of the "bog house." Note the original house may not have had a true back door.

Other Cape Cod Towns with Historic Cape Cod Houses

Wander around the Cape as Timothy Dwight did almost two hundred years ago and it becomes obvious that numerous old distinctive Capes in a variety of sizes and shapes are still standing. Each town, from the tip in Provincetown to the canal in the Sandwich/Bourne area has well-documented and excellent examples of this architectural style. Follow along as we visit a variety of Capes in the towns of Chatham, Orleans, Brewster, and Dennis.

Orleans

Orleans, located at the inside elbow of the Cape, and originally part of Eastham, has harbors both on Cape Cod Bay and the Atlantic Ocean. With a rich maritime history, Orleans, like the surrounding towns, has a long architectural record. There are literally hundreds of properties, many of these Capes, which have been identified and researched with regard to their history. There are several communities within the town and each has its own collection of old houses. One such group of homes is illustrated here. Fisherman or farmer, these are the basic homes of the settlers more than two and half centuries ago.

This half Cape, seen at present and in two black and white images a century old, is one of three houses in this neighborhood in Orleans. Little changed over two centuries, this house is now surrounded by trees.

Nearby is this three-quarter Cape, which also has several additions to the rear.

This old three-quarter Cape, with several additions to the rear, also has the barn still standing in close proximity.

Another three-quarter Cape, this house is located on a shady lane.

Nestled among fruit trees, the third house—former residence of Abner Snow—was significantly altered more than a century ago. Originally a full Cape, the house was cut in half and one section was moved north to Eastham. What remains is this half Cape with an atypical dormer. This house may be the oldest of the three since part of its framing beams and boards came from a fort built in Eastham in 1644.

Chatham

Chatham, located at the outside elbow and the southeast tip of the Cape, was first settled by the English in 1665 (the Prence House in Eastham was built in 1644). It was visited as early as 1606 by Samuel de Champlain, but after skirmishes with the Native Americans, he departed the area. A prosperous community that was involved in fishing and whaling, there are a considerable number of eighteenth-century buildings still standing. Many of these are Capes, as well as larger two-story colonials. Now a very popular tourist destination, Chatham still exudes old Cape charm, with its quaint harbors, the lighthouse, and its architectural heritage.

Hidden down a sandy lane in Chatham is this full Cape. In the old image, note the unusual addition extending to the left of the house. In the present day image, the house, used primarily as a summer residence, has been expanded for modern living. The front door, with distinctive moldings and sidelights, is basically unchanged.

With views looking over Oyster Pond in Chatham, this half Cape, built in 1740, has additions to both sides of the house, as well as a garage to the far left. Well maintained, note the typical sparse trim and batten door.

Brewster

West of Orleans and found along the north shore of Cape Cod on the King's Highway (6A), Brewster is well known for its many antique homes. Although there are numerous Capes similar in style to those on the Outer Cape found along the highway and throughout the town, many of the older homes are two-story colonials often referred to as "ships captains" houses. Brewster is unique in that it may have the greatest number of these homes, but it is the only town on Cape Cod without its own harbor. Two centuries ago, the owners of these large colonials would leave on extended sea voyages that would take them away from the town for numerous months. Many of these captains' homes are well maintained and are now inns and bed and breakfasts that attract visitors to spend time in a house built more than two centuries ago. The owners of the less ostentatious one-and-a-half-story Cape homes were farmers, fishermen, tradesmen, and businessmen—many of whom never left town. Side by side, Cape and colonial, these historic homes are still standing after many generations. Many of the Capes are still private residences, yet some have become antique and art galleries. The following homes are just a few that one will find while riding along historic Route 6A.

Originally built in Harwich, this half Cape house was moved to Brewster and expanded. The house has retained much of its original fabric.

Larger than your typical half Cape, this home has windows on the two sides that are more characteristic of a full Cape. Additions to the rear have expanded the size of the house. A barn on the property is of the same vintage as the house and now functions as an antique gallery.

This full Cape, built nearly two centuries ago, has more room on the second floor. Notice the distance between the top of the window and the roofline; this extra height results in more livable space. Several additions have produced a more modern home. On what was once a property that may have included as much as forty or fifty acres, a functional barn remains that at one time contained farm implements and animals.

Nearly three centuries old, these two classic full Capes are partially hidden from the street by trees.

Brightly colored, this full Cape, which is now a residence and art gallery, was once a store and may have been a stop on the stagecoach route.

Almost one hundred and fifty years old, this half Cape is found on a quiet side road.

Dennis

Dennis, in the Mid-Cape region, is one of three towns (the other two are Yarmouth and Barnstable) that front on Cape Cod Bay on the north shore and Nantucket Sound/Vineyard Sound on the south shore. Maritime activities played a major role in the town's industry, as clipper ships were built in Sesuit Harbor on the north shore. Before the railroad (mid-1800s), sailboats from other nearby harbors would race to and from Boston, delivering trade goods. Houses were built centuries ago that reflected the capability of these mariners. As in Brewster, there are many large colonials, as well as countless well-maintained Capes. The antique Capes are found primarily in two neighborhoods: on the north shore, along the King's Highway and in an area called Quivet Neck; and on the south shore, along the Bass River and in the Old Historic District. Ride along the roads in those areas and you will see some of the following homes.

Built in 1795, this full Cape shows more detail than similar houses on the Outer Cape.

A present day view of Sesuit Harbor looking south. Nowadays, large modern houses are built near the beach; centuries ago, dwellings would be constructed away from the beach in protected, sheltered areas. Some of the houses seen in these photographs can be found in the treed area to the east (left in photo) of the harbor.

Just a short distance down the same street is this second full Cape, which was built in 1790. The black and white image was captured more than ninety years ago. Closer examination of the front of the house reveals functional, curved door shutters, a five-panel fan light, and dentil molding.

Nearby is this half Cape, built in 1760, that has the typical clapboards on the front and shingles on the other walls.

This historic house was built by captain Theophilus Baker in 1801 and is now maintained by the Dennis Historical Society. Antiques, glassware, and tools are on display.

Built in 1836, this three-quarter Cape has been enlarged with additions to the rear of the house and a bump out on the side.

This antique Cape has three front windows in an unusual arrangement.

A classic full Cape behind a white picket fence.

A full shed dormer has been added to this Cape built in 1744.

The Vincent House (1672) may be the oldest house on the Vineyard. It was moved to this location in Edgartown after many years near the local harbor.

The Islands

South of Cape Cod, two islands, Martha's Vineyard and Nantucket, were both settled by the English before 1650. Steeped in maritime history, both islands were involved in whaling and fishing, and numerous architectural gems were built. Some were Capes and are still standing today. What is interesting is that with the decline of the whaling industry in the mid-nineteenth century, many houses were "flaked" (broken down) and carried on barge to Cape Cod. Many Capes remain on both islands and can be seen as you roam the back roads. The following images are just a few of the Capes found on both islands.

Compare this Edgartown half Cape with similar houses and note that the door is more commonly found on the left side. The number "10" represents the address; the "1840" over the door the date of construction. The white chimney topped with a black stripe was originally supposed to indicate Tory sympathizers—but built sixty years after the revolution, here it would seem to be more decorative.

A similarly designed half Cape found along a back road in West Tisbury.

Another Edgartown Cape, in this case a three-quarter, with an addition to the left. Built in 1849, note the unusual trim above the door and windows.

White houses with black shutters, no matter what size or style the dwelling is, constitute the most common paint scheme in Edgartown. The two chimneys are not located at the peak of the roof, and an overhang over the front door makes this house distinctive.

Two full Capes in Edgartown have similar dormers on the front roof.

Sitting on a hill and looking towards Menemsha Harbor is this full Cape. The front batten door, with two lights, has plain trim and a four light transom above it.

Across island in Vineyard Haven is this similar full Cape. Through the years, several additions have been added to both sides of the house.

On the eastern shore of Nantucket is the village of Siasconset; this map shows most of the original old homes. The community began as a fishing village in the 1670s. The cottages, smaller than other homes discussed in the book, were built from shipwrecks that washed up on the nearby shores. Timber and wood were at a premium and everything and anything possible was used to build these houses. In the late eighteenth century, this quaint collection of cottages became a resort destination. The circle at the bottom left of the map is the flagpole that greets visitors to the village. The colored dots indicate houses whose images are included here (courtesy of LOC).

SHELL STREET

CENTER STREET

BROADWAY

BANK STREET

NEW STREET

PUMP SQUARE

PARK LANE

FRONT STREET

N
W E
S

One of the oldest and largest of the original houses in the village of Siasconset is the Captain Valentine Aldrich house. Quickly recognized as a Cape because of its basic design characteristics, it is not until the winter when you observe that there is only one window on each side of the door. Built in 1733, the house was designed and constructed to fit the needs of the owner. It is identified on the map with the red dot.

Compared to other Cape-style homes, the cottages in the village of Siasconset are smaller versions of this architectural design. Auld Lang Syne, identified by the yellow dot, is seen in both summer and winter. Note the batten shutters and door. The drawings were part of a Library of Congress survey from about eighty years ago.

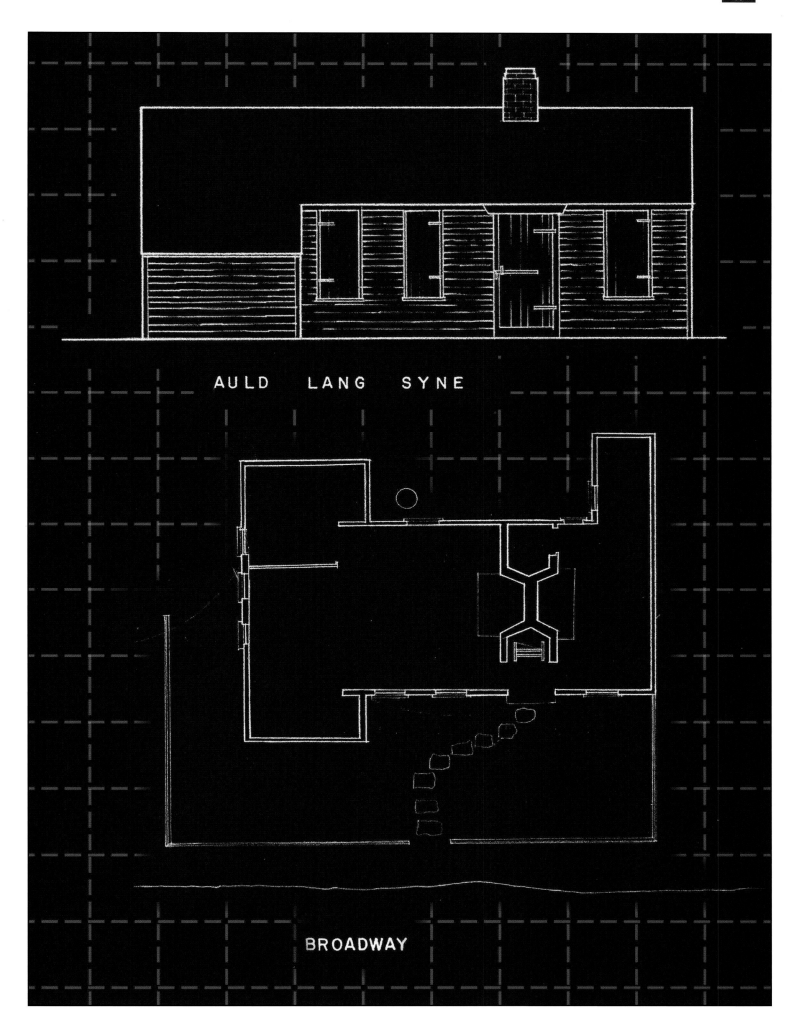

AULD LANG SYNE

BROADWAY

Just outside the village is this house; more architectural detail can be seen in the winter image.

This cottage, identified on the map by the green dot, is nearly totally hidden by flowers in the summer. Both the house drawing and the floor plan provide insight as to the actual structure of the cottage (*plan courtesy of LOC*).

This cottage, as the sign says, was built in 1734 and has an addition to the rear.
It can be located on the map as the house with the orange dot.

With the prosperity that came as a result of the whaling
industry, many homes in the town of Nantucket were more like
mansions. Some old two-story colonials remain, but there are a
significant number of Federal and Greek revival houses. On some
of the side streets, it is possible to locate a number of old Capes.
These two half Capes are neighbors on the same street.

Greek Revival

After the American Revolution (1780), the influence of Great Britain drastically declined in all aspects of the lifestyle of the people in the New World. Architecture was one area of significant change. In the middle of the eighteenth century, archeologists and architects were finally able to study and examine in detail the buildings of the first Republic—Greece. With the support and enthusiasm of Thomas Jefferson, who introduced Greek revival architecture to America, major construction projects, including the U. S. Capitol, involved this new building style. Banks, mansions, university buildings, and churches all emulated a style found in Greece thousands of years ago. Unfortunately, as we discussed earlier, with lack of information regarding the development of minor architecture in England, specifically what would become the Cape Cod cottage, relatively little is also written about the smaller Greek revival homes built on the Cape. People looking for an alternative to the Cape Cod house style, could now build a home in the Greek revival style. Turn the house around, place the off-set door on the gable end, add some trim reminiscent of a Greek temple around the door and on the corner boards and now you have the latest architectural style (Greek revival). As the population increased and more people lived near the center of town, the residents may not have been involved in agriculture or farming, but rather in some form of fishing. Located next door to each other, these Greek revival homes, built as much as two centuries ago, reflect the change that occurred in American architectural style. Although the Cape Cod cottage was still being built, there were now alternatives to the style of houses available. The following images show some of houses built across the Cape in the Greek revival architectural style.

More than a century ago, this family in Eastham posed for a group photo in front of a house that shows the influence of Greek revival architecture. The door has been moved to the gable side of the house. Note the trim around the door, the half circle vent under the peak of the roof, and the horizontal treatment of the roofline.

Looking west on Commercial Street in Provincetown, a Greek revival cottage can be seen on the corner of the street in the distance.

This house in Truro has a door on the gable end but shows little evidence of Greek revival influence (*courtesy of LOC*).

Compare these two houses, one in Eastham and the other in Harwich. Both are Greek revival homes but differ in their trim and windows. Corner boards may be narrow as in a traditional Cape-style house or wide as paneled pilasters in a Greek revival; an attic vent or window found in the pediment (the triangular area from the peak of the roof to the bottom of the roofline) is another difference.

This Greek revival house in Orleans has the door offset and a short horizontal roofline. Note the distance between the top of the first-floor windows and the bottom of the roofline, which translates into more headroom on the second floor. There are also rarely seen boards, "eyelids," which extend out above the windows.

Now an art gallery in Wellfleet, this house was originally built on Billingsgate Island and moved to this location sometime in the late 1800s. There are several interesting aspects to this façade: the first-floor window replacing two original windows (you can see the angled "eyelids" where the original windows were located), angled boards above the windows, and the gingerbread trim along the roofline. It is believed that the house was originally built in the early 1800s.

Brightly painted, this Greek revival house has wide column-like pilasters, a temple-like trim around the door, six over six panes in the windows, and side lights adorn a four-panel door.

Conclusion

From what began centuries ago in Europe as a basic cottage to what we now recognize as the Cape Cod house, this dwelling has become an indelible architectural style from coast to coast. Modified and adapted, mass-produced, or custom made for more than three hundred years, this has been one of the most common and popular architectural styles in the country. Its name may be Cape Cod, but this residence can be found everywhere.

Even though books concerning history and the years gone by may create a sense of nostalgia, the future of the Cape Cod house is bright. Architects and builders are increasingly amending this architectural style for the next generation. Having started in the New World ten to twelve generations ago, the Cape Cod house design is ready for the next century.

Windmills played an important function in the lifestyle of the early settlers.
This mill, the oldest on the Cape, is found in Eastham.

Bibliography

These are just a few of the many books that are available and some of the ones I used as research material for this project about the Cape Cod house design. Most of these books are of a historical perspective and many were published more than a half-century ago. For the enthusiast, there are also numerous new titles involving the modern design of this architectural style.

Doane, Doris. Drawings by Howard L. Rich. *A Book of Cape Cod Houses* (Old Greenwich, CT: The Chatham Press, Inc., 1970).

Foster, Gerald. *American Houses, A Field Guide to the Architecture of The Home* (Boston, New York: Houghton Mifflin Company, 2004).

Gitlin, Jane. *Updating Classic America Capes* (Newtown, CT: The Taunton Press, 2003).

Haas, Irvin. *America's Historic Houses and Restorations* (New York, NY: Castle Books, 1966).

Harris, Richard. *Discovering Timber-Framed Buildings* (Buckinghamshire, UK: Shire Publications Ltd., 2006).

Kelly, J. Frederick. *Early Domestic Architecture of Connecticut* (New York, NY: Dover Publications, Inc., 1952).

McAlester, Virginia and Lee. *A Field Guide to American Houses* (New York, NY: Alfred A. Knopf, 2003).

Nutting, Wallace. *Massachusetts Beautiful* (Framingham, MA: Old America Company, 1923).

Poor, Alfred Easton. *Colonial Architecture of Cape Cod, Nantucket, & Martha's Vineyard* (New York, NY: Dover Publications, Inc., 1932).

The Preservation of Historic Architecture, The U.S. Government's Official Guidelines for Preserving Historic Homes (Guilford, CT: Department of the Interior; The Lyons Press, 2004).

Robinson, Albert G. *Old New England Houses.* (New York, NY: Charles Scribner's Sons, 1920).

Schuler, Stanley. *The Cape Cod House, America's Most Popular Home* (West Chester, PA: Schiffer Publishing Ltd., 1982).

Schuler, Stanley. *Saltbox and Cape Cod Houses, 2nd Edition* (Atglen, PA: Schiffer Publishing Ltd., 2000).

Whiffen, Marcus. *American Architecture Since 1780, A Guide to the Styles* (Cambridge, MA: The M.I.T. Press, 1979).

Williams, Henry Lionel and Ottalie K. *Old American Houses, How to Restore, Remodel, and Reproduce Them,* (New York, NY: Bonanza Books, 1957).

Index